I0051099

Scalability and Realtime for Data Warehouses and BigData

(2nd Edition)

Pedro Furtado

Copyright © 2015 Pedro Furtado

All rights reserved.

ISBN: 9892050436
ISBN-13: 978-9892050430

DEDICATION

This book is dedicated to the most precious things in my life, my two children Pedro and Diogo. They helped me a lot, and they deserve all my help and support. They had to endure some extended periods without their dad, which allowed me to enhance my knowledge, write and complete the publication of this book.

CONTENTS AT A GLANCE

Preface 1

1. Warehouse Architecture and Scalability 9

2. Scalability Architectures 27

3. Scalable Query Processing 39

4. Partitioning for Scalability 53

5. Concurrent Workloads 71

6. Realtime Scalable Data Warehouse 77

7. Modern Scalability Frameworks 87

8. References 103

TABLE OF CONTENTS

Preface 1

1. Warehouse Architecture and Scalability 9

    1.1. Types of Applications 9

    1.2. Multi-dimensional Data Model 11

    1.3. Star Schema..13

    1.4. Decision Support Benchmark 15

    1.5. Star Schema Benchmark 19

    1.6. Data Warehouse Processes...20

    1.7. Scalability, Realtime and BigData 23

2. Scalability Architectures 27

    2.1. Parallel versus Distributed Processing 28

    2.2. Scalability, Parallelism and Concurrency 28

    2.3. Parallel Architectures 33

3. Scalable Query Processing...39

    3.1. Parallel Query Processing 39

    3.2. Query Processing with Horizontal Intra-Query Parallelism 43

    3.3. Chunk Processing...47

    3.4. Optimal Replica Placement..49

    3.5. Testing On-Demand Processing...51

    3.6. Further Readings 52

4. Partitioning for Scalability 53

    4.1. Partitions and Chunks 53

    4.2. Partitioning for Data Lifecycle Management...................56

    4.3. Workload-based Partitioning 58

    4.4. Workload-Join Partition&Place (P&P)......................61

    4.5. Using Workload-based Partitioning...........................66

    4.6. Co-located Partitioning for Dependent Relations 67

    4.7. Brief Experimental Analysis......................................68

    4.8. Further Reading...69

5. Concurrent Workloads 71

    5.1. Handling Concurrent Workloads 72

    5.2. Cyclic Query Processing 73

    5.3. Operators Sharing..74

6. Realtime Scalable Data Warehouse 77

    6.1. RealTime Data Warehouses......................................77

    6.2. Data Transformation 79

    6.3. Loading and Querying..80

    6.4. Total Scalability 82

    6.5. Query Results Merging Details..................................82

    6.6. Conclusions and Further References...........................85

7. Modern Scalability Frameworks 87

    7.1. MapReduce 89

7.2. Scalable Data Processing on Hive 91

7.3. Brief Results with Hive 92

7.4. NoSQL Data Stores 94

7.5. Exemplifying NoSQL with Cassandra 96

7.6. Realtime Scalable Analytics 98

7.7. Conclusions 99

8. References 103

About the Author

Pedro Furtado is Professor at University of Coimbra UC, Portugal, where he teaches courses in both Computer and Biomedical Engineering. He has more than 25 years experience in both teaching, doing research and supervising industry projects. He has a broad interest in computer science subjects, with the main focus being on performance and scalability qualities of systems. Pedro applied these qualities in data warehousing and analytics, bigdata, data mining, cloud, IoT and realtime systems. He also works in assistive technologies, applying mobile and internet-of-things technologies to healthcare scenarios. Pedro has more than 150 papers published in international conferences and journals, books published and several research collaborations with both industry and academia. In the last years, Pedro has spent time as visiting scholar in some prestigious universities in the world, and collaborating with non-profit institutions. Besides a PhD in Computer Engineering from U. Coimbra (UC) (2000), Pedro Furtado also holds an MBA from Universidade Catolica Portuguesa (UCP) (2004).

The knowledge that Pedro Furtado transmits through this book is the result of more than 15 years of research done by him in the area of data warehousing, scalability and analytics.

List of Acronyms

DBMS	Database Management System
RDBMS	Relational Database Management System
DW	Data Warehouse
SM	Shared-Memory Systems
SMP	Symmetric Multiprocessor Systems
SE	Shared-Everything Systems
SN	Shared-Nothing Systems
SD	Shared-Disk Systems
ACID	Atomicity, Consistency, Isolation and Durability
CEP	Complex Events Processing
OLTP	Online Transactional Processing
OLAP	Online Analytical Processing
IaaS	Infrastructure-as-a-Service
PaaS	Platform-as-a-Service
SaaS	Software-as-a-Service
DW	Data Warehouse
DSS	Decision Support Systems
NoSQL	Not-only-SQL

Pedro Furtado

Preface

The amount of data recorded, processed and managed has augmented at huge rates as the web age progressed, and as organizations became increasingly sophisticated and shifted from slow reaction times to acting quickly and proactively. The web increased dramatically the number of transactions and the speed at which transactions are done.

Technologies and mechanisms evolved to handle the scalability and realtime requirements of the new context. There were advances in hardware and software, but also in the way data processing systems are designed. Data warehouses are the large repositories of historical data that needs to be processed, managed and analysed efficiently.

This book describes data warehouse solutions to handle scalability and realtime needs of modern contexts. The mechanisms that should be used for scalability are studied, including foundations and most recent approaches that are also covered in the book. The topics of bigdata and the use of bigdata technologies in the context is also introduced.

The book can be used as part of a Graduate Course Curriculum, as a reference for researchers working on the theme or by practicing engineers in both integrators and companies commercializing systems for efficient and scalable data management. It can also be used as a reference on parallel/distributed databases in an undergraduate course. It assumes basic familiarity with computer and software systems, databases and SQL, the kind of knowledge that would be acquired in introductory courses in those subjects.

Organization of the book

The rest of the book is organized as follows: Chapter 1 reviews the traditional architecture of a data warehouse, the repository that needs to be scalable in order to handle large amounts of data and queries efficiently. Chapter 2 discusses scalability, focusing on hardware and software architectures that allow a computerized system and data management software to handle larger amounts of data efficiently. Chapter 3 discusses the approaches followed by data management systems to provide scalable query processing, including on-demand parallel query processing. Chapter 4 concentrates on partitioning approaches. These approaches divide the data and assign the parts to different processing units, to make it possible to restrict the data that must be accessed to answer a query and for parallel processing. In that chapter we describe the types of partitioning that can be used and how they work. Solutions to provide scalability to large numbers of sessions concurrently querying data are discussed in chapter 5 on scalability of data warehouses to concurrent workloads. Given the increasing trend to shorten the cycle between the time data is recorded and when it is used as knowledge, Chapter 6 describes the limitations of traditional data warehouse designs regarding realtime and how to achieve both near-realtime and realtime scalable processing over the data warehouse. Finally, we describe modern frameworks for scalability in Chapter 7. In that chapter we explain how Hadoop, MapReduce and Hive can be used as underlying infrastructure and tools for scalability.

After reading this book, the reader will understand the main concepts and mechanisms behind scalable data management. The reader will understand not only the foundations of scalable processing over data management systems, but also the various approaches to solve data management scalability and realtime issues.

1. Warehouse Architecture and Scalability

Data warehouse is the name commonly given to a repository of historical data that is organized in a way that facilitates analysis. The data may be about past sales transactions, user clicks or all indexed pages and words in the web. The data that is needed for reasoning and use in other processes has to be collected, readied and queried in the repository. The term 'Data warehouse' is usually associated with the 'Decision Support System', since it is used to analyse data and to take decisions based on the results of the analysis. The term "Data Warehouse" is also associated with 'Online Analytical Processing' (OLAP), which refers to analysing data online that is organized logically as a multidimensional dataset.

A naïve data warehouse organization could be a simple log or set of logs recording all the data that needs to be analysed, but most frequently the data will be loaded into a database repository for efficient storage and use. This chapter describes the model that is typically used to organize and reason about data in data warehouses.

1.1. Types of Applications

Applications do not all share exactly the same workloads and requirements. In particular, a typical classification separates decision support applications (associated with terms such as "data warehouse" and "online analytical processing" - OLAP), and transactional applications (a.k.a operational systems or "online transaction processing systems" - OLTP). The requirements of those are quite different, but scalability is very important in both cases.

Transaction processing (OLTP) applications are the applications that serve everyday business processes, recording every transaction that occurs in a business. They are also known as operational systems. There may be thousands of sessions simultaneously accessing data servers, for searching, browsing, inserting, updating or deleting data. Each interaction is a short transaction, many times accessing or inserting specific rows in tables. E-commerce sites are an example of transactional system. Visa-card payment machines and ATM machines are other examples of human-computer interfaces associated with online transactions processing. Transactional systems are characterized by many short interactions that must guarantee reliability. There may be tens of thousands or even millions of simultaneous payments, money transfers, balance queries and other transactions happening simultaneously. The data servers to support those interactions must ensure security, ACID properties and be ready to serve multiple simultaneous sessions. There are specialized structures and approaches to speedup access in transactional systems. For instance, indexes are important for accessing individual rows of tables that are requested in short transactions, e.g. a row on an accounts table accessed by account-ID, or a list of the ten last transactions linked to that account.

Scalability in OLTP applications should focus on how to allow tens or hundreds of thousands of simultaneous transactions to commit and return answers in less than a second each. The slowest transactions should not take more than 2 to 5 seconds, in order to allow seamless interactivity with users. This can be a challenging objective, but there are mechanisms to provide that degree of scalability.

Decision support or online analytical processing (OLAP) applications have different characteristics. Instead of thousands of small transactions, they provide support for a fewer number of simultaneous business data analysis and reports. They can produce charts and interactive exploration of business-related data for decision support and to discover important knowledge. For instance, if we collect every visa-card payment that happens in a country into a data warehouse, or every click stream interaction from weblogs and every sales transaction in Amazon site, this will allow managers to explore and search for specific knowledge of interest in the data. Those warehouses will probably grow immensely as they accumulate data, and will require optimization techniques for accessing enormous amounts of data in few seconds and archiving approaches. Scalable OLAP data servers should provide quick answers to queries that would otherwise take a lot of time to run, due to the need to scan and process enormous amounts of data.

The multidimensional model is the most frequently used conceptual organization of data in data warehouses. The next sections detail the model and its implementation in database systems.

1.2. Multi-dimensional Data Model

A multidimensional data model is a model of data that considers a set of variables, attributes or properties as dimensions against which to analyse a dataset. The dataset is made of a set of data items or tuples. The set of independent dimensions to consider is first identified in the dataset metadata. A very simple example is given next to describe the approach. Figure 1.1 shows an example weblog entry. The entry includes the IP address of the client (remote host) which made the request to the server, the userid of the person requesting the document, the date, time and timezone, the resource that was requested, the status code returned by the server, and the size of the object returned to the client.

127.0.0.1   user-identifier   carl   [14/Oct/2013:12:05:13   -0700]   "GET /text.txt HTTP/1.0" 200 1471

Figure 1.1 – An example web log entry

In this case we could consider as dimensions the Requester, Date-time and the Resource that was requested. The resulting multidimensional model has three dimensions (Requester, Date-time, Resource). The Requester may be considered to have attributes IP and User-Identifier, Date-time can be considered to have one attribute for each date and time constituent, and the Resource can be considered as having two attributes– the resource identifier and the size of that resource. The resulting dimensions and the instance values for the tuple of Figure 1.1 are:

Dimension Requester(IP and User-Identifier) = (127.0.0.1, carl)

Dimension Date-time(day,month,year,hour, min, sec, timezone) = (14,Oct,2013,12,05,13,-0700)

Dimension Resource(identifier, size) = (/text.txt", 1471)

These dimensions and their attributes are the perspectives over which the dataset will be analysed. For instance, we may want to determine how many resources were accessed by user carl (Requester) on a specific day (Date-time), or we may want to know the fraction of requests that returned a server error. Queries combine the dimensions to compute some desired analysis.

Besides dimensions, there are also measures, which are the properties and quantities that are measured (analysed). In the previous example, those were the status and the number of requests. In order to compute the number of resources accessed by carl in one day, all that is needed is to compute how many times the specific combination of dimension attribute value 'carl' and the specific day occurs (each web-log entry of 'carl' for the desired day is one recorded access). As another case, to count the number of times a server error status appears in the dataset, there needs to be a measure associated with status. The final multidimensional model is represented next, where X stands for 'combine', D stands for 'dimension' and M stands for 'measure'.

D(Requester) X D(Date-time) X D(Resource) = M(status)

The multidimensional model is therefore an interpretation of the dataset. The dataset may remain as it is and be processed by some custom code or by some software framework that is able to read the data as weblog entries and do the computation, or it can be subject to pre-processing in order to organize it in a way that facilitates its use for analysis.

One common approach is for the data to be loaded into a database schema with relational tables defined according to the dimensions and measures. Queries can then be expressed in SQL and processed efficiently by the database query processing engine. The process of changing the organization of the data to load it into the data warehouse is called extract-transform-load (ETL). Extraction means to extract data from the data sources (weblog), transformation accounts for transforming the weblog into the adequate format (requester, date-time, resource, measures), and loading refers to loading the formatted data into the final structures that will hold them (database tables). Besides the database itself, there are various tools to specify and operate extraction and transformation and to invoke loading into the final structures (database).

1.3. Star Schema

The previous example can be expressed as a star schema in a database. Figure 1.2 symbolizes a typical relational organization of a data warehouse star schema Kimbal [40]. Figure 1.2a shows the structure, with a central fact table (F) and 4 dimensions (a). Figure 1.2b shows a corresponding example. The schema shown in Figure 1.2b records sales of products in places (stores) along time. It may record every sales transaction or summarize sales of products by some time granularity.

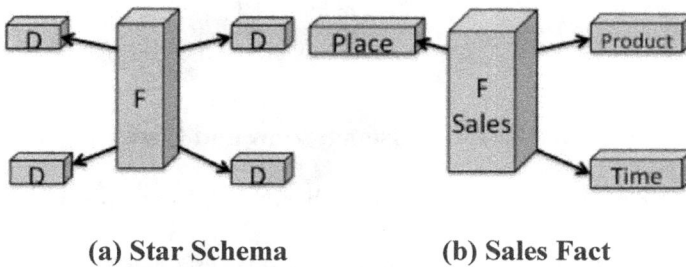

(a) Star Schema   **(b) Sales Fact**

Figure 1.2 – Star Schema: structure and example

Figure 1.3 illustrates a table creation pseudo-script for this kind of schema. Notice the fact table referencing each dimension table (foreign keys). The star schema in that figure is a representation of the multidimensional dataset shown in Figure 1.3b. The axis of the cube in Figure 1.3b are the dimension tables of Figure 1.3a, and the cube cells contain measures from the fact. The query is also shown in Figure 1.3b. It computes total sales per product brand per month.

```
Create table product {          Create table time {
product_key,                    time_key,
brand,                          year,month,
type,                                  day
cost                            }
}
```

```
Create table salesFact {
product_key references product,
time_key references time,
sales measures
}
```

(a) Create Table Pseudo-Script

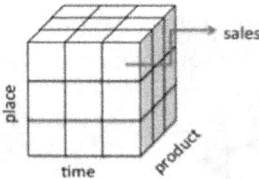

```
Select brand, month, sum(sales)
From [dim(i)], fact
Group by brand, month
```

(b) Multidimensional View and Query

Figure 1.3 – Creating Star Schema with Foreign Keys

Exercise: As an exercise, you can try to draw the database tables for the weblog example, and the SQL queries for obtaining the number of entries for user 'carl' in a specific day and for obtaining the fraction of times requests resulted in a server error status.

While we have given simple examples, a typical data warehouse in some large company can have a large number of star schemas, many facts and dimension tables. Some of the dimension tables, such as Time, can be shared by multiple stars.

In order to further illustrate the concept of data warehouse, the next two sections describe examples of data warehouse that are frequently used by researchers to experiment with new designs. They are decision support benchmarks whose schemas and queries illustrate sales data warehouse repositories. In the first case we have a database schema that holds past sales data, while the second case is a star schema derived from the first one.

1.4. Decision Support Benchmark

TPC-H [68] is a benchmark that simulates a Decision Support System a.k.a. Data Warehouse. It is used mostly to evaluate performance of database engines when processing online analytic processing workloads. We summarize its schema and queries in this section, and its deployment in a relational database system. The reader is encouraged to try out with the benchmark, since it is very easy to install and test using the documentation and resources that are provided [68].

A typical benchmark to evaluate database systems is composed of at least a schema (the structure of the data), a data generator or data generation rules, a workload (the set of queries or analysis that are tested), and the definition or rules and a procedure to run the tests of the workload against the schema. The system to be evaluated is called the 'System Under Test' (SUT).

The TPC-H benchmark defines two very important elements in a database, the schema and the workload. The schema is the structure of tables that will hold the data, while the workload is the set of queries that are submitted against the data for retrieving answers. The TPC-H schema represents a data warehouse repository for a commercial order-processing environment. It stores data of a fictitious multinational importer and retailer of industrial parts and supplies. Customers and suppliers for this retail business can come from different parts of the world (regions) and different countries (nations) within those regions. Customers place several orders and each order can contain many different part purchases from different suppliers at different prices (lineitem). The list of parts and suppliers are connected by a table (partsupp), to indicate which specific parts were supplied by each supplier. Figure 1.4 summarizes the schema diagram for TPC-H, which is detailed in [68].

This is not a "pure" star of multidimensional schema. We could vaguely say that Lineitem, Orders and PartSupp are "degenerated" facts linked to each other, while Part, Supplier and Customer are dimensions. The following are SQL commands that create the schema of TPC-H.

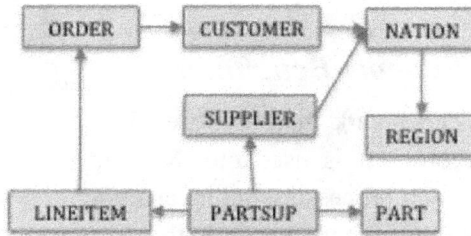

Figure 1.4 – TPC-H database schema

```
CREATE TABLE TPCD.NATION ( N_NATIONKEY  INTEGER NOT NULL,
           N_NAME      CHAR(25) NOT NULL,
           N_REGIONKEY  INTEGER NOT NULL,
           N_COMMENT    VARCHAR(152))

CREATE TABLE TPCD.REGION ( R_REGIONKEY  INTEGER NOT NULL,
           R_NAME      CHAR(25) NOT NULL,
           R_COMMENT    VARCHAR(152));

CREATE TABLE TPCD.PART ( P_PARTKEY    INTEGER NOT NULL,
           P_NAME      VARCHAR(55) NOT NULL,
           P_MFGR      CHAR(25) NOT NULL,
           P_BRAND     CHAR(10) NOT NULL,
           P_TYPE      VARCHAR(25) NOT NULL,
           P_SIZE      INTEGER NOT NULL,
           P_CONTAINER CHAR(10) NOT NULL,
           P_RETAILPRICE DECIMAL(15,2) NOT NULL,
           P_COMMENT    VARCHAR(23) NOT NULL );

CREATE TABLE TPCD.SUPPLIER ( S_SUPPKEY    INTEGER NOT NULL,
           S_NAME      CHAR(25) NOT NULL,
           S_ADDRESS    VARCHAR(40) NOT NULL,
           S_NATIONKEY  INTEGER NOT NULL,
           S_PHONE     CHAR(15) NOT NULL,
           S_ACCTBAL    DECIMAL(15,2) NOT NULL,
           S_COMMENT    VARCHAR(101) NOT NULL);

CREATE TABLE TPCD.PARTSUPP ( PS_PARTKEY   INTEGER NOT NULL,
           PS_SUPPKEY   INTEGER NOT NULL,
           PS_AVAILQTY  INTEGER NOT NULL,
           PS_SUPPLYCOST DECIMAL(15,2)  NOT NULL,
```

```
                    PS_COMMENT    VARCHAR(199) NOT NULL );

CREATE TABLE TPCD.CUSTOMER ( C_CUSTKEY    INTEGER NOT NULL,
                C_NAME      VARCHAR(25) NOT NULL,
                C_ADDRESS    VARCHAR(40) NOT NULL,
                C_NATIONKEY  INTEGER NOT NULL,
                C_PHONE     CHAR(15) NOT NULL,
                C_ACCTBAL   DECIMAL(15,2) NOT NULL,
                C_MKTSEGMENT CHAR(10) NOT NULL,
                C_COMMENT   VARCHAR(117) NOT NULL);

CREATE TABLE TPCD.ORDERS ( O_ORDERKEY    INTEGER NOT NULL,
                O_CUSTKEY     INTEGER NOT NULL,
                O_ORDERSTATUS  CHAR(1) NOT NULL,
                O_TOTALPRICE   DECIMAL(15,2) NOT NULL,
                O_ORDERDATE   DATE NOT NULL,
                O_ORDERPRIORITY CHAR(15) NOT NULL, -- R
                O_CLERK      CHAR(15) NOT NULL, -- R
                O_SHIPPRIORITY  INTEGER NOT NULL,
                O_COMMENT     VARCHAR(79) NOT NULL);

CREATE TABLE TPCD.LINEITEM ( L_ORDERKEY    INTEGER NOT NULL,
                L_PARTKEY    INTEGER NOT NULL,
                L_SUPPKEY    INTEGER NOT NULL,
                L_LINENUMBER  INTEGER NOT NULL,
                L_QUANTITY    DECIMAL(15,2) NOT NULL,
                L_EXTENDEDPRICE DECIMAL(15,2) NOT NULL,
                L_DISCOUNT    DECIMAL(15,2) NOT NULL,
                L_TAX       DECIMAL(15,2) NOT NULL,
                L_RETURNFLAG  CHAR(1) NOT NULL,
                L_LINESTATUS  CHAR(1) NOT NULL,
                L_SHIPDATE    DATE NOT NULL,
                L_COMMITDATE  DATE NOT NULL,
                L_RECEIPTDATE DATE NOT NULL,
                L_SHIPINSTRUCT CHAR(25) NOT NULL,
                L_SHIPMODE    CHAR(10) NOT NULL,
                L_COMMENT     VARCHAR(44) NOT NULL);
```

The workload of TPC-H represents analysis that include:

• Analysis of Pricing and Promotions;
• Management of Supply & Demand;
• Management of Profit and Revenue;
• Customer Satisfaction Studies;
• Market Share Studies;
• Shipping Management Analysis;

The benchmark also defines a set of tests/runs that need to be followed to evaluate a system under test, using a strict set of rules. It uses as primary performance metric, indexed by the database size, the composite query-per-hour performance represented as QphH@Size, where 'Size' represents the size of data in the test database.

Performance analysis with TPC-H involves running a set of 22 queries and refresh sets, following some rules defined in the benchmark documentation. The tests can be done using varied scale factors. The scale factor (SF) defines the approximate size of the database that will be generated. For instance, SF=10 means that the data set will have approximately 10 GB of data.

The following query (Q10) is provided as an example of the 22 TPC-H queries. The queries are defined in detail in [68]:

Q10
```
select
        c_custkey,c_name,sum(l_extendedprice * (1 - l_discount
        n_name,c_address,c_phone,c_comment
from
        customer,orders,lineitem,
        nation
where
        c_custkey = o_custkey
        and l_orderkey = o_orderkey
        and o_orderdate >= date ':1'
        and o_orderdate < date ':1' + interval '3' month
        and l_returnflag = 'R'
        and c_nationkey = n_nationkey
group by
        c_custkey,
        c_name,
        c_acctbal,
        c_phone,
        n_name,
        c_address,
        c_comment
order by
        revenue desc;
```

1.5. Star Schema Benchmark

The Star Schema benchmark [53], or SSB, is derived from TPC-H. It was devised to evaluate the performance of database systems when dealing with a star schema and queries over it. Once again, we encourage the reader to try out with this benchmark, since there are many resources online to install and run it.

The Star Schema Benchmark, as the name itself implies, has a star organization. Figure 1.5 is an illustration of SSB entities. SSB records sales on a Lineorder table referencing Customer, Supplier, Part and Date (dimensions to which lineorder fact links).

In SSB, queries are organized into four flights of three to four queries each [53], with the following contents:

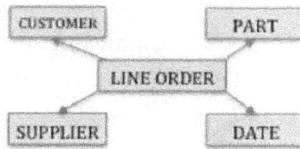

Figure 1.5 – SSB database schema

•Query Flight Q1. This query measures the revenue increase from eliminating various ranges of discounts in given product order quantity intervals shipped in a given year. Query Flight Q1 has three queries with different select filters;

•Query Flight Q2, has restrictions on two dimensions. The query compares revenues for certain product classes and suppliers in a certain region, grouped by more restrictive product classes and all years of orders;

•Query Flight Q3, has restrictions on three dimensions. The query retrieves total revenue for LINEORDER transactions within a given region in a certain time period, grouped by customer nation, supplier nation and year. There are four queries in this Query Flight;

•Query Flight Q4, provides a "What-If" sequence of queries that might be generated in an OLAP style of exploration. Starting with a query with rather weak constraints on three-dimensional columns, we retrieve aggregate profit grouped by year and customer nation. Three queries in this Query Flight modify the predicate constraints by drilling down to find the source of an abnormality;

The following are examples of query Q1.1 and Q2.1. More details are available in [53].

Q1.1
select sum(lo_extendedprice*lo_discount) as revenue
from lineorder, datewhere lo_orderdate = d_datekey
and d_year = 1993and lo_discount between1 and 3 and lo_quantity < 25;

Q2.1
select sum(lo_revenue), d_year, p_brand1 from lineorder, date, part, supplier where lo_orderdate = d_datekey
and lo_partkey = p_partkey and lo_suppkey = s_suppkey and p_category = 'MFGR#12' and s_region = 'AMERICA'
group by d_year, p_brand1 order by d_year, p_brand1;

1.6. Data Warehouse Processes

As discussed in the previous sections, data warehouses get their data from data sources. Data sources include operational systems – systems recording events and doing day-to-day transactions – and other sources (e.g. weblogs). The operational data is extracted, transformed and loaded into the data warehouse. This process is called extract-transform-load (ETL). In a typical data warehouse, ETL runs periodically. It is necessary to identify new data that must be loaded since the last load. Figure 1.6 summarizes the parts of the system.

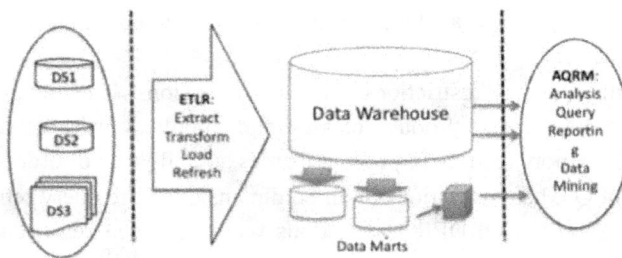

Figure 1.6 - Elements of a Data Warehouse

In Figure 1.6, operational databases and other sources provide input for periodic data extraction. The data is then incorporated into the warehouse. Depending on the context, the data warehouse may be loaded daily or weekly, or even monthly. In data warehouses that are not designed for realtime, it is important to do ETL periodically instead of as soon as the data appears, since extracting data from operational systems impacts the performance of those systems, and operational systems are critical to businesses. Periodicity also makes clear what data is available for analysis. For instance, if the data is loaded every night, users know that they are analysing up to the last day.

Periodic loads are fine for most data warehouses, but quick and proactive reaction is necessary in other contexts, giving rise to realtime warehouses. If we want to detect intrusions or to have almost instant feedback on accesses to a new webpage, the period between two consecutive ETL integration processes must be small. The challenge in realtime warehousing is how to integrate the data immediately or almost immediately as it appears in operational systems, and simultaneously to limit the consequences of continuous extraction in operational systems and data sources in general.

Another challenge in data warehousing is how to integrate data and analyse it with small latencies even when the data is huge. The next paragraphs briefly review the integration steps in a data warehouse, and their scalability and realtime needs.

For extraction, the system needs to have a way to know the update set, representing the new data entered and modified in the operational systems since the last extraction happened. Change Data Capture (CDC) mechanisms [75, 52, 39, 61, 56] are a common way to do that efficiently. Usually, a log registers information on the insertions and modifications that happened so that, when the update set is to be extracted, the log is used to feed the update set to the next step. [71] reviews extraction techniques that can be adapted for near-realtime ETL. Specifically, the online transactional system can be enriched with an enterprise application integration middleware that essentially sends each data change to the ETL process as it occurs; another alternative is to use a log sniffer that can parse or scrap the log between two timestamps, redoing the changes in the data staging area; triggers capture data changes and write modifications to special tables, files or memory structures, for the extraction step to use; Finally, another alternative is based in timestamping all tables, in order to be able to identify and extract only the data between two timestamps.

After extraction, the next step is transformation. The extracted data goes into a staging area, the place where transformation and loading happens. Transformation refers to modifying data. There are data sources and source data formats, and there is a data warehouse schema format. The source data is transformed into the warehouse schema for being incorporated into it. Many operations may be required in the transformation phase, such as selecting only certain columns to load, translating coded values, encoding free-form values, deriving calculated values, sorting, looking up values, merging and splitting columns, aggregating, generating surrogate-key values, applying any type of simple or complex data validations. Transformation can be implemented in a staging area – an intermediate location where the data is handled - or in a database, after loading the data. ELT refers to this alternative of extract, load and then transform the data.

The loading step concerns taking the transformed data and loading it into the data warehouse schema. Loading also involves refreshing the database structures with the new data. But a typical data warehouse has several star schemas instead of only one. For instance, a company warehouse may include a large number of star schemas, including one for analysing sales of products, another for analysing sales per customer, one more for pricing analysis, one for supply-chain analysis and many other.

It is also typical to have summarized information as well as detailed one in a data warehouse. For instance, besides recording each individual sale, that information is summarized into hourly sales and daily sales, hourly sales by brand and daily sales by brand, monthly totals and many others. Some database engines include materialized views as table structures that maintain and refresh those summary tables automatically.

Loading and refreshing concerns loading the data warehouse star schemas with new data, and refreshing all other structures that are related with the warehouse. This process takes time, and also impacts analysis performance if done simultaneously with querying. Finally, it may result in incoherent analysis results if the analysis is done as the data is being updated.

The final step that we should consider is analyzing, querying, reporting and mining the warehouse data. The process of querying the warehouse data is often called Online Analytical Processing (OLAP) and Reporting.

Performance is a relevant issue in many practical data warehosues. It is not the same to query a data warehouse with 1 GB, 100 GB or 1 TB. And yet, users most frequently want to have interactive-time answers to their queries and want their report to be ready quickly, regardless of the size of the data. In other words, there is a major scalability need in many big data warehouse contexts, to be able to deliver results quickly.

1.7. Scalability, Realtime and BigData

Scalability is necessary when a certain hardware and software setup will not be sufficient to handle large loads. This can happen when one or a few conditions happen: the amount of data in the data warehouse can be too big to be processed efficiently without massive parallelism (Volume), data may need to be loaded and/or analysed at high rates (Speed), or there can be a large number of simultaneous sessions querying the database (Competition).

Scaling refers to improving the capacity of the server(s) to handle requests, so that a delta increase in server(s) capacity will handle a gamma increase in the amount of load. There are two major forms of scalability, scaling-up and scaling-out. Scaling-up refers to upgrading the hardware of a server machine (e.g. more memory, faster disk sub-system), so that it becomes more powerful and capable of processing more load. From now on we focus on the other type of scalability, which is scale-out. Scale-out refers to adding servers to increase the amount of resources that can process the load, and dividing the load into the servers.

Scale-in is the opposite process, whereby the number of servers is decreased because the load also decreases.

The most desirable form of scalability in environments with a certain degree of uncertainty in what concerns Volume, Speed or Competition is semi-automated (or even automated) scalability. Semi-automated scalability refers to systems that are able to scale with simple configurations, typically because they have a set of automated procedures to rebalance data and load.

In order to scale out, it is necessary to bring-in scalability software architectures, in the form of mechanisms that allow the queries to run fast in spite of the size of the data. Partitioning and parallelism using a set of commodity servers are typical scalability mechanisms that we will talk about in the next chapters. Scalability is very frequently necessary in data warehouses, to guarantee that queries are processed efficiently. However, it can also be necessary in all stages of the ETL pipeline. If the processing requirements are huge or due to the realtime/short latencies requirements, it may be necessary to have huge computational power on those stages as well.

As we described earlier, realtime concerns being able to integrate source data into the data warehouse with short latencies. The time between an event happening and when the recorded data on that event is integrated into the data warehouse and analysis-ready should be minimal for a data warehouse to be considered realtime.

There is a significant current industry momentum for having realtime business intelligence affecting day-to-day business decisions and operations. For instance, if a new product or service is a top-seller or top-looser, the company may want to react quickly, adjust pricing, promote the product or service, suggest to other consumers, integrate new information into recommendation systems quickly. Likewise, if a Telco company is loosing clients, it may want to detect that quickly and offer discounts on calls to you and to your friends, or analyse the data to detect opportunities to stay more competitive while decreasing prices.

In order to have realtime, there need to be answers regarding how to extract data from the operational system very frequently or as soon as it is generated, with minimal interference with operational processing, and how to transform the data with minimal latency and maximum throughput. Loading, refreshing and querying are also critical processes. Loading can be significantly delayed in traditional data warehouse architectures for at least two main reasons: if indexes, constraints and other auxiliary structures are kept during the loading process, then there will be a slowdown of the process, since updating those structures takes time and must be done for each row that is inserted/modified/deleted; loading is also severely slowed when running simultaneously with query sessions being submitted and processed by the system; Conversely, query response times can be increased during online loading.

Refreshing refers to the need to update a large number of redundant structures holding data, such as indexes, aggregated summaries, materialized views and others. Those redundant structures result in better performance, since they allow queries to be answered against them or data to be accessed faster through them, instead of processing a large amount of base data. But, in realtime warehousing, the process of refreshing those also competes for the same resources as query processing, and increases loading plus refreshing times.

In the next chapters of this book we will discuss scalability and realtime architectures and mechanisms.

When talking about scalability, we should also mention the topic of BigData, since these two topics are very closely related, and scalability is necessary to handle big data. Big Data is both a buzzword and a very important concept that indicates the direction to be followed in industry and in research for building scalable data management and processing for the next decades. A simple characterization of BigData is known as the three V's: Volume, Velocity and Variety, to which a fourth V was also added by some: Veracity. BigData is about how to deal efficiently with information that can be huge in volume, may arrive at a high rate and may have various formats. A significant part of the information may be unstructured or semi-structured instead of adhering to the traditional well-defined schema.

Most of the mechanisms investigated before for scalable processing are useful for handling BigData in general. Partitioning and parallel processing are useful for handling large volumes of data, while realtime approaches and complex event processing are able to deal with high data arrival rates. More importantly, the BigData movement has given emphasis to the development and use of scalable BigData processing platforms, and noSQL engines that do not require a totally predefined schema, this way providing better support to variety.

2. Scalability Architectures

Scalability can be defined as the capacity of some system to handle growing amounts of work in a capable manner, or its capability to be enlarged to handle larger amounts of work comfortably [5]. The last decades have seen an exciting revolution in terms of research on data management infrastructures for scalability. Concepts such as BigData and Cloud Data Management became mainstream. The community started to view automatic scalability as a major objective.

Scalability is most frequently obtained by means of parallel architectures and minimization of processing bottlenecks in those architectures. Parallel hardware and software architectures are used repeatedly in different environments, for instance in parallel relational database engines, map-reduce frameworks or cloud virtualized environments. In this chapter we describe the foundations of parallel architectures.

2.1. Parallel versus Distributed Processing

Different people sometimes have different meanings for the same terms, in particular the terms parallel and distributed processing can raise some confusion. That is why we start this chapter by providing one possible definition for the term "parallel processing", a definition that we use all over the book:

Given some workload, parallel processing refers to the use of multiple processing units (PU) to divide the workload, so that parts of it will be processed in each computation unit. A processing unit is some piece of hardware that is able to process tasks given to it. The processing units are then said to process in parallel. Examples of processing units are microprocessor cores, multiple microprocessors, racks in a multi-rack server, or servers in a multi-machine cluster or in a data centre. Individual machines are frequently called nodes in the case of multiple servers. The workload can be a single task that is divided into sub-tasks, or many tasks that are routed to different computation units, or some mix of those two.

The term "Distributed processing" has some overlap with this definition in the case of multiple servers. A distributed system is made of networked computers that communicate and coordinate their tasks, and either the machines may be allocated to independent work or they can cooperate to solve some large computational problem.

In this book we discuss scalability using the term "parallel", corresponding to the definition that we gave above. Therefore, parallelism is a divide-and-conquer approach that can run in any architecture that offers multiple processing units, whatever they are.

2.2. Scalability, Parallelism and Concurrency

As already noted here, scalability can be defined as the capacity of some system to handle growing amounts of work in a capable manner, or its capability to be enlarged to handle larger amounts of work comfortably [5]. Parallelism is an important tool for achieving scalability of data processing. It enables the divide-and-conquer paradigm, where a problem is sub-divided into smaller sub-problems that are solved in parallel and then combined to give a solution to the original problem. Parallel data management solutions do this by dividing the data and/or processing over a set of processing "nodes". Figure 2.1 is an example of the divide-and-conquer paradigm. A dataset is divided into three parts and each one is assigned to a different node. If the nodes all have the same computing capacity, the data is already locally in each node, and a task that needs to run over the initial dataset can be parallelized without limitations, we can expect the task divided into the nodes to run about three times as fast as the initial task. Linear speedup is defined as a system running n times faster when it runs n processing nodes than when it runs in only one node. In practice, additional startup, data exchange and results merge overheads can contribute to worse performance than that theoretical linear speedup. But the reverse is also true in practical systems. It is possible for the system to exhibit a super-linear speedup. For instance, if the solution with a single node or a few nodes has to page data to disk that doesn't fit into memory, perhaps more nodes will each have a much smaller amount of data that fits entirely into memory, resulting in a super-linear data processing speedup. This can be summarized as stating that, beyond saturation, systems slowdown significantly. Saturation is defined as the point after which resources needed for processing (e.g. memory or processing cores) are nearly 100% utilized. In those situations, adding processing units or memory will result in significant performance improvement.

Referring to the same Figure 2.1, another illustration of scalable operation can be seen if the system takes more or less the same time to process the task when we place the same amount of data in each of the three nodes that we had in the single node. The size of the data increased threefold, but the data processing resources also increased threefold.

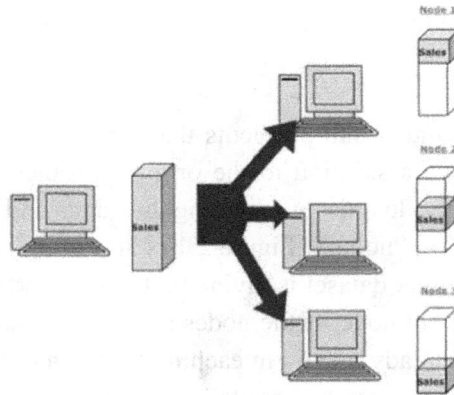

Figure 2.1 – Data Divide-and-Conquer

The concept of embarrassingly parallel is also of interest to parallelism and scalability. According to parallel computing terminology, an embarrassingly parallel workload or problem is one that can be divided into a number of parallel tasks with little or no effort, and there is no dependence between processing units for processing the data. If a problem is embarrassingly parallel, we can achieve high degrees of speedup and scalability with parallelism.

One simple case where the way we place data determines if we achieve embarrassingly parallel processing or not over relational data, is the parallel processing of a join between two relations where the rows of both relations are divided into many computer nodes. The dependency between processors can be minimized if we hash-partition both relations by the join attribute (equi-partitioning) during data placement. If the data is already hash-partitioned when the queries are going to be processed, each node will only have to take care of the rows stored locally when it processes a join. But, as we will see in a later chapter, it may be impossible to guarantee that every possible join will be equi-partitioned in a schema.

Another overhead that adds to the parallel query processing part in a parallel database management system is results merging. In spite of those limitations, a significant level of parallelism and therefore of scalability is possible in query processing in data management systems.

Another concept that is very important in parallel data management architectures is load balancing. A parallel system should balance processing adequately to take maximum advantage of parallelism. Load balancing concerns getting sure that each processing unit shares the load in a manner that is proportional to its performance index. The performance index is a relative measure of performance between the processing units. If the processing units are homogeneous, this means that every processing unit should share exactly the same load. A very simple pattern to achieve load balancing in any system is the on-demand or pull pattern. The idea is that, instead of some complex way to plan a system for load balancing, it can be obtained by processing units pulling tasks when they are going to have spare processing power. We will discuss this pattern in a later chapter.

One important aspect of any parallel architecture is that the slowest components dictate performance. For this reason, when analyzing the advantages and disadvantages of architectures, it is most important to identify the major bottlenecks that they possess.

Parallelism can be obtained using different alternatives, and resulting in different advantages. While in Figure 2.1 parallelism was obtained by means of dividing the data into multiple nodes, in Figure 2.2 queries are divided into a number of nodes, each having the full amount of data. The effects are also different in the two cases. In data division, a query running alone may be expected to complete its execution much faster than in a single node system (response time reduction), while in the second case, each query running alone will take the same time to execute as in a single server system (it has to go through the same amount of data), but the system will be able to process multiple queries much faster than if all queries would run against the same resources (throughput maximization). In both cases throughput (number of queries that the system can serve per unit of time) is expected to improve significantly when compared with a single node system.

Figure 2.1 and Figure 2.2 illustrate nodes as computers, but nodes over which to implement parallelism do not need to be separate servers. Nodes can be cores in multicore processors, or processors in multiprocessor systems, servers or a mix of all the previous alternatives. The nodes in those figures can be seen as an abstract processing unit concept that can be realized using different alternatives.

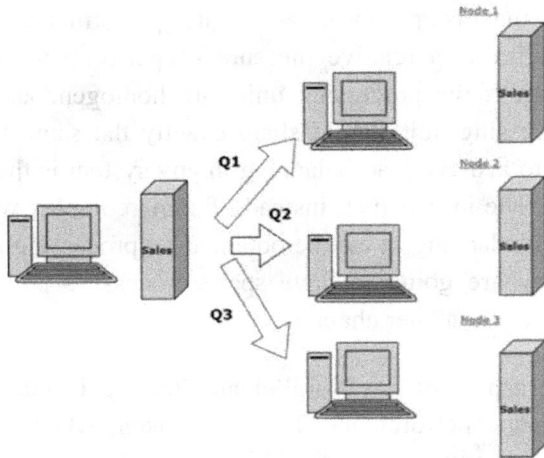

Figure 2.2 – Query Workload Divide-and-Conquer

There are important differences when we consider different scenarios. The performance overhead of exchanging data between nodes is very different if nodes are servers or cores in a multi-core processor. The data may be physically divided into different disks in multi-server systems, or partitioned in the same storage medium for multi-processor or multi-core architectures to divide the load among them. In this second case it is possible that a disk controller be a bottleneck when it has to serve multiple requests simultaneously.

Traditionally, database systems are designed for concurrent execution of multiple transactions. The fact that a system is able to run multiple transactions simultaneously does not mean that it will guarantee a larger throughput. For instance, consider a single processing unit (e.g. a single-core processor) constantly switching execution among a set of three transactions, executing a portion of each. If each transaction has the amount of work W to be done and the extra work overhead due to switching as many times as necessary to end the work concurrently is S for each transaction, all transactions will end after 3W + 3S. To this overhead, we should then add overheads related to ensuring correct concurrent execution and concurrent access to resources (e.g. locking and latching). If, on the other hand, the transactions are executed sequentially, then the first transaction will end after W work is done, the second after 2W and the third after 3W, therefore it seems preferable to have sequential execution than to execute the transactions concurrently. However, there are two main reasons to execute concurrently. The first one is that the amount of work that transactions need to do is not homogeneous, therefore concurrent execution allows fast transactions to end quickly instead of waiting possibly large amounts of time until some slow-executing transaction ends. The second one is that there are usually more than one processing unit in current architectures (e.g. multi-cores, multi-processors or multiple machines) and I/O systems, buses and protocols are also optimized to serve multiple requests quickly.

2.3. Parallel Architectures

Parallelism is the omnipresent pattern in scalable data management and processing. For instance, parallelism is crucial to deal with huge data warehouses. Data warehouses serve as support for the storage of historical business data and for multidimensional data analysis over that data. Although data warehouse sizes range from a few megabytes to huge giga- or tera- bytes, they are expected to compute reports and return results to ad-hoc queries almost interactively. Given huge data sets, it is necessary to apply a set of techniques to speedup processing over those warehouses. But while materialized views [60] or specialized indexes [51, 7] can improve performance, they are not enough to guarantee interactive response times to all queries. Both indexes and materialized views efficacy are restricted to some query patterns that are in accordance with those structures.

Intra-query parallelism offers scalability by cutting either or both the query and data into pieces and assigning those pieces to different processing units. Given several computing units, most data query operations can be processed efficiently in a parallel manner. Data partitioning [70] is crucial in this process, since it offers the adequate chunk sizes for dividing and feeding them into processing units.

There are different nomenclatures for the basic models by which a parallel system can be designed, and the details of each model vary as well. Parallelization of data storage and processing follows one of the following basic patterns: shared-nothing, shared-disk, shared-memory and hybrid. Current state-of-the-art servers come with multiple processors, which enables multi-core and multi-processor architectures to become commodity.

A parallel system has a set of basic elements: the processing unit (P), disk storage (D) and memory (M). The generic types of parallel architectures include shared-memory, shared-nothing, shared-disk and hybrids [15][21].

The first model is Shared Memory (SM) or Shared Everything (SE). Figure 2.3 illustrates that architecture. In this architecture, all the processors use the same memory address space and peripheral devices. In terms of software for data management and processing, a single application is present which must parallelize processing into multiple threads or processes in order to utilize all processors.

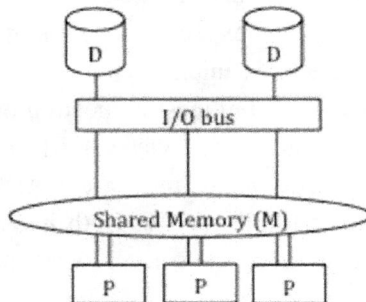

Figure 2.3 – Shared Memory Pattern (SM)

Another term commonly associated with SM architectures is Symmetric multiprocessing (SMP). SMP systems are defined as tightly coupled multiprocessor systems that share a set of homogeneous processors. All processors share a common set of resources (memory, I/O and so on) and are connected using a system bus. The identical processors are connected to a single shared memory and are controlled by a single OS instance. Currently, most multiprocessor systems use an SMP architecture. In the case of multi-core processors, each core is seen as a separate processor for the SMP architecture.

Shared-memory (SMP) architectures usually have few processors or cores. One important point in favour of this architecture is that the same programming paradigm is used as in single-processor machines. The operating system deals with shared memory concurrency and dynamic load balancing issues, which refers to dynamically distributing the tasks among the processing units. On the other hand, scalability is constrained in these architectures due to the limit on the number of processors/cores. The number of processing units is pre-defined and also constrained by the characteristics of the shared system bus.

The Shared Nothing (SN) pattern, illustrated in Figure 2.4, is made of multiple processing nodes, where each one owns its processing unit (P), memory (M) and I/O devices (D). Nodes communicate using message passing through an interconnection network. More generically, a processing node can have one or more processors and/or I/O devices. Contrary to the shared-memory architecture, in shared-nothing architectures each node runs a separate copy of a Database Management System (DBMS). This separate copy is the node component of the shared-nothing DBMS.

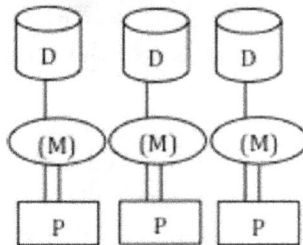

Figure 2.4 – Shared-Nothing Pattern (SN)

In terms of hardware, shared-nothing architectures are cheap, and the number of nodes can be scaled easily. It is possible to make an SN with commodity nodes linked using a local area network. A huge number of nodes can be used because they do not share any other resources except the network.

Shared-Nothing (SN) systems can be made with low-end clusters with commodity computing nodes and an ordinary network, or top-performing clusters made of high-end shared-memory machines. The disadvantages of SN architectures include the need to develop specialized applications in order to run in the SN infrastructure, and the performance limitations concerning data exchange between SN nodes. Data needs to be exchanged between nodes, but this requires going through network interface cards on both sides and the network. Due to these limitations, SN systems should take care concerning data placement, query processing and load-balancing.

When comparing shared-memory (SM) systems to shared-nothing ones (SN), we note that SMs share everything - memory, DBMS, stored data - , while SN clusters need to pre-distribute the data, exchange it on-the-fly, and run a software that distributes, synchronizes and manages execution of the whole cluster. But, on the other hand, the achievable degree of parallelism with SN nodes is conceptually unlimited, since nodes can always be added. The design of the system should take into consideration the amount of data and application requirements.

The shared-disk architecture (SD), illustrated in Figure 2.5, is made of multiple loosely coupled processing nodes, similar to SN. But the nodes access a global storage system. Any node accesses this storage system through an interconnection network, which should be fast and allow high bandwidth.

The sharing of disk storage in shared-disk systems (SD) has the advantage over shared-nothing systems (SN) that the data is not divided into nodes, instead it is stored centrally in shared storage. But this creates a critical constrain and severely limits scalability, as all the nodes need to access and share bandwidth from the same interconnection network and disks. For scalability, both the interconnection network and the disk sub-systems need to provide a large bandwidth. Technologies such as RAID and firewire should be used to achieve those performance capacities.

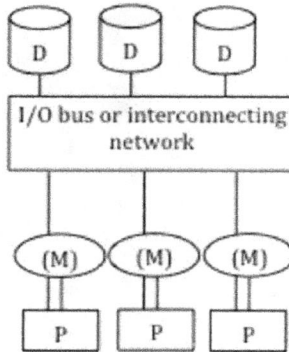

Figure 2.5 – Shared-Disk Pattern (SN)

Today, hybrid architectures are the most usual in practical deployments, as multi-core and multiprocessor systems gradually become a commodity. Many of those shared-memory machines are put together in an interconnected network of servers, resulting in shared-nothing environment with shared-memory nodes. Simultaneously, software is developed that can take advantage of both shared-disk centralized storage sub-systems and local storage units that may be used as very large disk caches for data.

Two major scalability options are followed. On one end there are expensive solutions using proprietary, specialized and highly optimized software on high-end servers with powerful multiprocessor machines, expensive storage and I/O sub-systems; On the other end there are low-cost systems, which are deployed as shared-nothing architectures using commodity low-end multiprocessors, open-source or middleware data processing software.

3. Scalable Query Processing

Parallel database systems offer a single query interface to the user. Once a query is submitted, it is parallelized into component per-node queries, submitted to each node and processed in parallel. It is necessary to re-write the query to obtain node queries, submit those node queries to each processor, collect the results in a merge node and return the result to the user or application that did the request. In this chapter we first describe how parallel query processing works, showing the alternatives. After reviewing parallel query processing we also describe in more detail parallel horizontal intra-query processing and on-demand chunk-based query processing. The last is an important pattern in most existing scalable data management solutions. All the discussions in this chapter are generic and could be applied to any particular system that would implement the concepts that are discussed here.

3.1. Parallel Query Processing

The path followed in a traditional standalone database management system from query submission to returning the results of the query goes through parsing, building of a logical query plan, producing alternative execution plans, evaluating the costs of each and choosing the least costly execution plan. Then the plan is executed. The query processor processes the data that is on disk and cache, computes the result and returns. Parallel query processing is very important even in standalone database servers, since most modern hardware are multi-core architectures. An execution plan can be parallelized, and parts of it ran in parallel using multiple threads. But it is also possible to parallelize by simply assigning different queries to different processors. The following are alternative parallel query processing mechanisms: inter-query, horizontal intra-query, vertical intra-query and hybrid. If we look at the problem from the perspective of data, the data can either be divided by the processors (physically or logically) or copied into all processor units. Queries can be sent to different processors each (inter-query parallelism), or re-written into queries that are sent to processors, each processing a portion (intra-query horizontal parallelism). A third choice is for a query execution plan to be split into parts that execute in parallel and pipelined fashion, different parts being assigned to different processors (intra-query vertical parallelism).

Figure 3.1 depicts intra-query parallelism with two choices of architectures, SN and SD. The figure shows the data that should be processed, how the data is partitioned, the queries and their shipping into processors for execution. In the SN architecture of Figure 3.1 (a), the data is partitioned physically into pieces that will reside in the individual disks (D) when it is loaded. At execution time queries are re-written to node queries that are dispatched to the nodes. Nodes execute the queries against their data and return results that are merged and returned to the user.

In the SD architecture of Figure 3.1 (a) there is no need to load the data into different nodes. The data resides in a single storage, but it should be partitioned, so that partitions are loaded into the individual memories (M) of individual nodes.

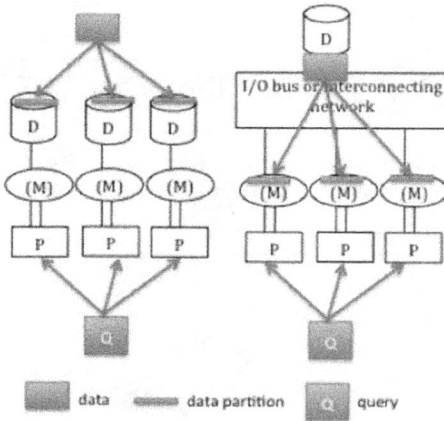

(a) SN architecture(b) SD architecture
Figure 3.1 – Intra-query Horizontal Parallelism (SN and SD)

Although in the most generic query cases it may be necessary to process the query in all nodes, if the data was partitioned based on a key that is used as a constraint in the query, it may be possible to access only one or a few nodes to answer the query. For instance, if the query accesses specific data rows concerning a specific day, and the days were used as partitioning keys, a single node may return the answer. This special case is explored in NoSQL systems that store the data based on a key-value pair. In those systems, retrieval using the get primitive is very efficient, since the data is stored indexed by the key and is also accessed by the key. In parallel NoSQL settings, nodes represent hash-key ranges, therefore a get request by a specific key value requires access to a single data node.

Figure 3.2 shows how inter-query parallelism can be obtained in both SN or SD systems. Each query is dispatched to a node and executes entirely in that node. Therefore, each node accesses all data and processes a query completely. Parallelism is achieved by having multiple queries execute in multiple nodes. This approach is very common when scaling webservers, where more than one webserver is setup and queries are load-balanced by those webservers.

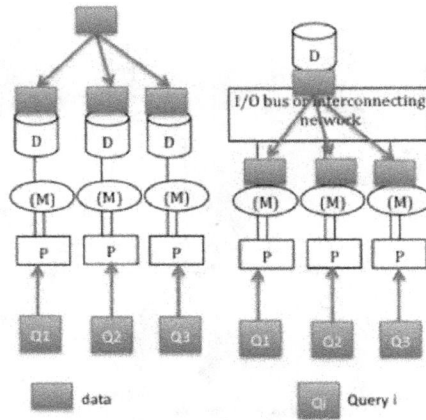

(a) SN architecture(b) SD architecture
Figure 3.2 – Inter-query Horizontal Parallelism (SN and SD)

Inter-query parallelism requires some form of scheduling of the queries into nodes following a load balancing policy. In round-robin if query *i* goes to server *j*, query *i+1* is assigned to server *(j+1) MOD servers*. Better but more complex policies assess server utilization and schedule queries to least loaded servers. Least-work-remaining scheduling either counts the number of queries currently running on a server, or the load on each server as a result of lower-level performance monitoring. Based on these measures, a new query is assigned to the least-work-remaining server.   The load of the servers can be evaluated using CPU or I/O use measurements.

In intra-query parallelism, a query can run about *n* times faster, but if there are multiple simultaneous queries submitted, they may all need to run over all nodes. On the contrary, in inter-query parallelism each query takes as much time as if it runs over one-node system, but the system will be able to process a larger number of queries, since each node will process a fraction of the queries.

Vertical intra-query parallelism is another kind of parallelism that can be used in multi-core architectures processing queries with complex execution plans. It divides a query into parts that are pipelined to answer the query. For instance, for a shared memory system with two cores to answer a query joining tables T1, T2 and T3, it is possible to have one core do the join between T1 and T2. The tuples resulting from this join are constantly fed to the second core, which joins it to the third table T3.

Relational Database Management Systems (RDBMS) must be adapted to the architecture in which they will run. In shared-memory inter-query parallelism architectures, each processing unit has an RDBMS process that is similar to a standalone RDBMS engine. It executes SQL statements using the same approach as normal uni-processor architectures, and communicates with each other by exchanging messages and data through shared memory. In shared-nothing intra-query parallel architectures, the parallel DBMS server is composed by a set of node DBMS components and a global component. The global component must parallelize the SQL queries and send the resulting sub-queries to execute locally at each node. Nodes exchange data and messages through the interconnection network. Some merger query must be prepared and executed on the results after the component nodes execute node queries. We discuss horizontal intra-query parallelism in more detail in the next section.

3.2. Query Processing with Horizontal Intra-Query Parallelism

Intra-query parallelism requires queries to be parsed, optimized and executed against all nodes. In order to process the intra-query parallelism using a middleware, queries are re-written into node queries and merge query, and then ran against the parallel system. Some central coordinator node will manage the execution, requesting execution of the parts in individual nodes and orchestrating the results merging in a merger node. In this section we illustrate how complex queries can be decomposed into a number of smaller sub-queries that will act on fragments independently, with significant speedup. There are many other references on intra-query parallelism that describe the kind of processing that we describe in this chapter, including (not exclusively) [24][2][62][92][93][94][95].

The illustration of Figure 3.3 concerns how a parallel query processing middleware processes queries in a shared-nothing node partitioned database. The data in the database is divided into the Executor nodes in the figure. A submitter node receives user requests, parses them and creates node queries that it sends to the executors. Node queries are normal SQL queries that are derived from the initial query to run on local databases on each node. Executors are standalone database engines that access their local database by submitting the node queries locally. It may be necessary for an Executor node to run multiple local queries and to exchange data in the middle of the query, in some defined order. The submitter node orchestrates all those operations and instructs Executors to do all the necessary processing and data exchange operations as needed. After all Executors have finished their parts, they route their results to a merger node. The merger node can be any node that is elected to merge the results from the Execution nodes into a final result. Typically, the merger node will have a database, the partial node results will be collected into that database and the merge query will also be a database query. For faster speeds, the merger may run an in-memory database.

Finally, a Manager node is needed to maintain a catalog of the system. New nodes contact the Manager for registry.

It is trivial to explain how a query retrieving a subset of the rows of a table is parallelized. Each node retrieves its part of the required data and forwards it to the submitter. In the next paragraphs we explain how aggregations, which are slightly more complex, are processed.

A relation R has a set of tuples. The symbol [] represents a set, T represents a tuple, so that [T] represents the set of tuples of R. Furthermore, "a" represents a value of attribute "a", and [a] represents a set of attribute values from a set of tuples.

Relation R is partitioned (divided) into n nodes. The subscript "i" in $[T]i$ represents the i-th node, therefore $[T]i$ represents the tuples in node i.

Consider three nodes, with the relation data divided into those three nodes. Consider the set of tuples [T] of relation R. then,

$$[T] = [T]_1 + [T]_2 + [T]_3 \tag{1}$$

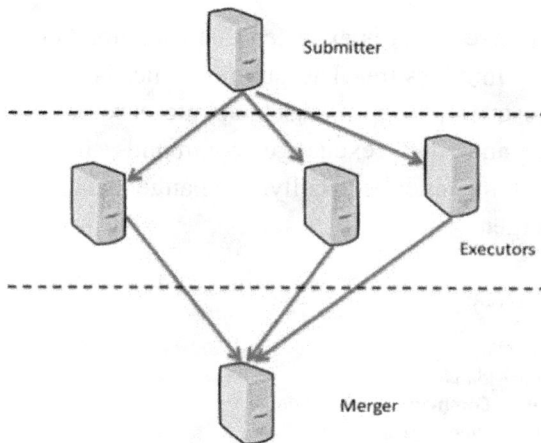

Figure 3.3 – Shared-Nothing Infrastructure for Intra-Query Parallelism

This means that a query selecting all tuples from R will concatenate the tuples coming from all nodes. This is the simplest query case that we described above.

A sum of some attribute over all tuples is computed as the sum of the sums of the tuples from each node,

$$SUM[a] = SUM[a]_1 + SUM[a]_2 + SUM[a]_3 \qquad (2)$$

The number of tuples is,

$$COUNT[a] = COUNT[a]_1 + COUNT[a]_2 + COUNT[a]_3 \qquad (3)$$

An average is computed as a sum of all tuples divided by the number of tuples,

$$AVG[a] = (SUM[a]_1 + SUM[a]_2 + SUM[a]_3) /$$

$$(COUNT[a]_1 + COUNT[a]_2 + COUNT[a]_3) \qquad (4)$$

In order to compute this average AVG[a], the partial query sent to all executor nodes needs to be modified to compute both SUM[a] and COUNT[a], and the merge query must do the above computation.

Figure 3.4 summarizes what is expected that each node do in the parallel query processing middleware. The submitter needs to parse and plan execution of the query, then it must generate a set of commands that include queries and data exchange commands for the executors. Executors submit the queries locally, exchange data and forward the results to the merger.

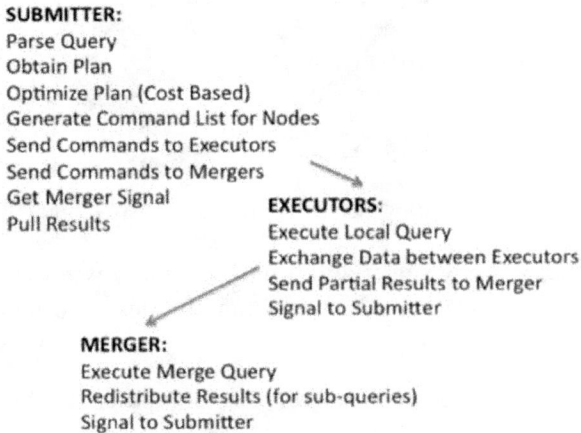

SUBMITTER:
Parse Query
Obtain Plan
Optimize Plan (Cost Based)
Generate Command List for Nodes
Send Commands to Executors
Send Commands to Mergers
Get Merger Signal
Pull Results

EXECUTORS:
Execute Local Query
Exchange Data between Executors
Send Partial Results to Merger
Signal to Submitter

MERGER:
Execute Merge Query
Redistribute Results (for sub-queries)
Signal to Submitter

Figure 3.4 – Horizontal Intra-Query Processing Steps

Figure 3.5 shows the generic pattern followed for aggregation queries, where each node needs to apply an only slightly modified query on its partial data (partial aggregation AggregPARTIAL()), and the results are merged by applying again a slightly modified query in the merging node (AggregMERGE()), against the partial results coming from the processing nodes.

The approach described above is not the only way to process queries using intra-query parallelism. A cost-based query optimizer can enumerate alternative plans that take into consideration the executor nodes and alternative parallelization algorithms for each operation. For instance, an aggregation grouping by a set of attributes can be done based on assigning the processing of the rows of each group to a specific node, based on hashing the group by attribute values. After generating multiple query processing plans, the optimizer would determine the best alternative for each query.

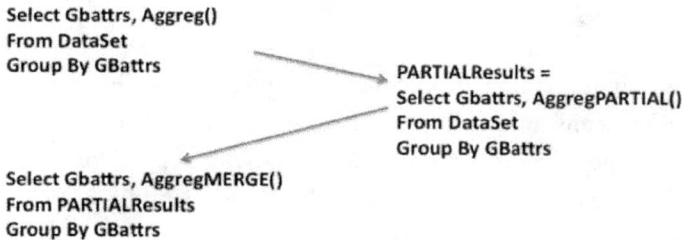

```
Select Gbattrs, Aggreg()
From DataSet
Group By GBattrs                           PARTIALResults =
                                           Select Gbattrs, AggregPARTIAL()
                                           From DataSet
                                           Group By GBattrs
Select Gbattrs, AggregMERGE()
From PARTIALResults
Group By GBattrs
```

Figure 3.5 – Typical Aggregation Pattern

The discussion in this chapter omitted difficulties that arise from the need to process joins over multiple relations in parallel partitioned settings. While most SQL operations are readily parallelizable with minimum data exchange requirements, the parallel join operator may require considerable data exchanges if the rows to be joined are not co-located or equi-partitioned (located in the same node). This is because the join must match rows from two data sets with the same value for a specific attribute. We discuss parallel join processing in a later chapter.

3.3. Chunk Processing

In order to achieve high degrees of scalability by means of parallelism, the data should be divided into chunks (equal-sized amounts of data). Those chunks are the units of parallelism whose processing can be assigned to different tasks, and they are also the units of parallelism that can be moved easily between nodes. For fault tolerance, they are the units of parallelism that can be replicated into multiple nodes as well. In this and the next sections we will describe how modern scalable data management systems process data efficiently using chunk-based on-demand approaches. A complete model and procedure for performance and availability-wise parallel warehouses that optimizes chunk-based placement and processing is described in [22].

We assume data is organized into chunks regardless of other data partitioning options (chunks may reside inside of partitions, which are then sets of chunks). If the data is partitioned based on some hash or interval criteria, chunks in a partition will obey to that criteria. Partitioning is described in a later chapter.

The fixed chunk size needs to be defined a-priori. If there were too many very small chunks, there would be a big extra overhead related to switching disk scans among chunks; If, on the other hand, the chunk was defined too large, we would not take full advantage of load-balancing opportunities and moving chunks would be harder. Chunks of 100 MB or 500 MB could be convenient sizes nowadays.

A chunk replica is a copy of a chunk, which resides in a different node from the one holding the original chunk. Given chunks, performance-wise chunk placement and replication is the process of determining how the chunks can best be placed to deliver the best possible efficiency, without copying every chunk into every node.

For the remaining discussion in this chapter, we consider a data warehouse star schema [41], since it allows us to illustrate and further clarify the concepts. The star schema has a huge fact table that is related to several much smaller dimension tables. When considering a parallel system, we apply Partition-and-Replicate algorithm [97], which results in partitioning the central fact table into multiple pieces that can be processed in parallel. In a shared-nothing environment, this corresponds to dividing the fact throughout the nodes. Therefore, the facts will be divided into chunks, and the chunks will be divided into nodes. Following this approach, most operations can proceed in parallel, including processing of joins in parallel.

Chunk-wise query processing considerations are not different from basic query processing over partitions [1, 24, 20], also described in the previous section on parallel query processing. If the dataset is divided into chunks, local node queries are executed against a number of chunks that are scanned in sequence. The submitter node instructs executor nodes to scan a number of chunks, and those nodes generate a result R(i) per set of chunks, which must be merged to obtain the final result. In on-demand load-balancing, as soon as a node ends processing chunks, it starts merging its local results and then sending the result to a merger node. When all nodes end processing all the chunks, the merger node applies the final merge query.

The chunk metadata is a simple structure with per-node information on the chunks that exist in the node, as shown in table 3.1. Given Nn nodes, the metadata structure has Nn cells, each with the identity of the set of chunks in that node. Chunk i is identified as ci in the table. Every 10 chunks are divided sequentially into the corresponding 10 nodes, until the last chunk c1010. Besides this division, replicated chunks are also present for fault tolerance and load balancing. Chunks have a primary node, but chunk replicas can reside in any other node.

node 1	node 2	...	node 10
c1	c2	...	c10
c11	c12	...	c20
...	...	...	
c1001	c1002	...	c1010
c2	c3	...	c1
c13	c14	...	c12
...	...	...	...

Table 3.1 - Chunk Metadata

Nodes consume their own chunks, after which they can start consuming replica chunks from other nodes that may be late processing their own chunks. The on-demand load-balancing algorithm, based on a Master node (which can be the submitter of the query), is shown in Figure 3.6.

This algorithm takes care of load balancing and fault tolerance issues automatically. If a node is unavailable, the nodes containing replicas will replace its processing. Nodes that had already ended their work for the query are also waken up if they have replica chunks of the failing node, in order to speedup the process.

3.4. Optimal Replica Placement

The default chunk placement strategy is to let nodes have approximately the same number of chunks (e.g. using random or round-robin assignment of chunks into nodes). A replication degree r means that there will also be r replicas of each chunk divided into different nodes. This replication serves load balancing and fault tolerance objectives. If nodes fail or are late, other nodes replace their processing.

Master Node:

Send to all nodes the query to run on chunks, and to the merger node the merger node query
tell Worker nodes to start on-demand requests for chunks
tell Merger node to wait for all worker nodes, execute merge at the end

While(there are still un-executed chunks in chunk metadata structure)
        Wait for requests from nodes
        If node still has chunks to process
        Tell node to process chunk
        Else if node has replica chunks not yet processed by their primary node
        Tell node to process replica chunk
        Else
        Tell node to merge partial results and send to Merger node

Worker Node:

While (master has chunks that node can process)
        Process requested chunk
        Tell which chunk is done to the master
Merge chunk results for those chunks that ran locally
Send result to Merger node

Merger Node:

Receive results from worker nodes
Apply merge query
tell master that Merge is done, result can be retrieved

Figure 3.6 – Load-Balanced On-Demand Processing

Load balancing is useful in the presence of heterogeneity. Since nodes ask for work (on-demand processing), slower nodes are automatically replaced by faster ones. Transferring chunks from one node to another during processing is assumed costly (it involves reading from storage, transferring, receiving and storing), therefore it is an important objective to maximize locality of access of chunks. For this reason, load balancing relies on chunk replicas that are already in the nodes.

The best load-balancing is guaranteed if nodes have all chunks, this being denoted as full replication. However, full replication is too expensive in terms of insertions and wasteful in terms of storage costs. Instead, the placement and number of replicas are optimized without the need for full replication. Furthermore, if the nodes are heterogeneous, then the placement can be unbalanced, in the sense that faster nodes (faster hardware) will have more chunks to process.

The performance of a node is defined using some benchmark, preferably a data processing benchmark. If node i takes time ti to run the benchmark, then we define the performance multiplier $p(i)$, $= ti(slowest)/ti(node_i)$.

A node with performance multiplier p should have p times more chunks than the slowest node. The chunk placement algorithm then does a weighted round-robin assignment of chunks to nodes.

The algorithm for replicating chunks should also guarantee that the replicas of primary chunks of a node are equally dispersed into all other nodes (or, for optimal performance, placement should be performance-wise). That way, if a node fails or is taken offline, the system will still be able to process queries efficiently, since all other nodes will be able to replace part of the processing of the missing node. A simple algorithm for replica placement is to replicate chunk x of a node i (x starting at 0) into node $(x+1)$ MOD N.

3.5. Testing On-Demand Processing

We briefly analyze experimentally the effects of heterogeneity, degree of replication, optimal chunk placement and replication policy using a simple experimental setup. The setup uses the TPC-H benchmark [68] with a scale factor of 10GB and running in 8 PCs (Windows 7, with 4GB RAM, 500 GB disks). To experiment with heterogeneity and load-balancing, we added an external load to four of the PCs in order to simulate an heterogeneous (or non-dedicated) environment. The extra load was based on executing TPC-H queries in round-robin fashion over a 1GB data set. The database engines were Postgres with the default configuration. The relations Lineitem and Orders were equi-partitioned on their join key, the remaining ones were replicated.

Figure 3.7 compares the performance (in queries processed per hour) of homogeneous chunk placement (homo) to that of chunk placement in accordance to the performance of nodes (perf-wise). The tests used replication degrees of 0, 2, 4 or full replication (all chunks replicated into all nodes). The performance of a single server setup is also shown for comparison. We can conclude that performance-wise placement improves the performance significantly when compared with homogeneous placement for this experimental setup, and this advantage decreases as the replication degree increases, as expected. In the extreme, if every chunk exists in every node (full-replication) and on-demand processing is used, then performance-wise placement is unnecessary, but full replication is costly in terms of insertions and storage.

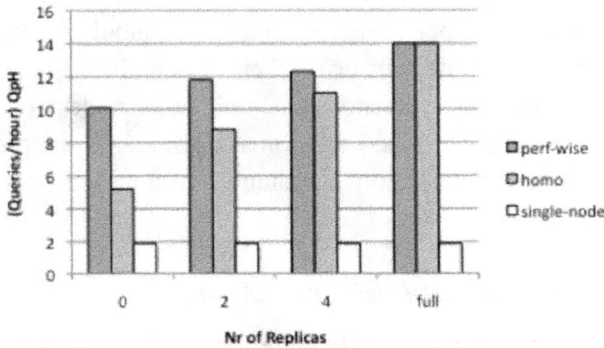

Figure 3.7 – Performance (QpH) versus Placement and Nr of Replicas

3.6. Further Readings

Parallel query processing in database management systems has been investigated thoroughly along the years, here we mention only a few. Already in 1978, Epstein et al. [92] discussed distributed query processing in relational database systems. Other references on parallel query processing include [93],[94][95][24][101]. The following two works discuss parallel database systems in general and the mechanisms used to parallelize and process [15][21]. Chunk-based parallel query processing with load balancing is discussed in [22], and replicated placement and processing in [23].

4. Partitioning for Scalability

Partitioning is an essential tool for obtaining scalability by means of parallel processing and assigning partitions to parallel resources. There are different partitioning approaches, focusing on different ways to deal with huge datasets. More than one partitioning approach can be combined in the same system to create an adequate way to deal with size. In this chapter we describe partitioning approaches. Other references on partitioning that discuss specific approaches are (not exclusively) [95][96][97][98][99][100][101][18][19][20][21][22][23] [24].

4.1. Partitions and Chunks

Partitioning or chunking is the process of dividing data into partitions or chunks that can be placed and processed autonomously. The data is a set of data items, and some property value of each data item – identifier - is used to determine the partition to which the data item is assigned. In relational databases the data is organized in tables, data items are individual tuples of the table and the property value is one attribute whose value is used to determine the partition to which it belongs. Partition sizes may be fixed or depend on the partitioning strategy used. In contrast, we define chunks as fixed-size pieces of data. It is also possible to define a partition as a larger unit of division that can hold many (fixed-size) chunks.

A partitioning strategy or policy is usually associated with partitioning. The following are common partitioning policies:

Hash – A hash is a function that is applied to an attribute value of some data (e.g. a row in a relational table) to determine which partition will the data will be put into. Given an attribute value x that identifies some data, a hash value y and a hash function h, then $y=h(x)$ will be the identity of the partition that will take the data. A simple example of a hash-function is the modulo of the division by some quantity. The quantity m will define the number of partitions that will exist, and $y = x$ mod m will indicate the partition into which the data with identifier x will fit into. For instance, a table row with identifier value 41 is placed in partition 1 by the hash function (mod 10) that defines 10 partitions.

Interval or Range – It is possible to define ranges of values that correspond to individual partitions. The dataset is partitioned by assigning the adequate partition to each data item based on the range to which the identifier belongs.

Round-robin – round-robin partitioning does not take into account the actual value of the identifier. Instead, it assigns data items to partitions in sequential order.

Random – similarly to the round-robin partitioning, random partitioning does not use the value of identifiers. But, instead of assigning data items to partitions sequentially, it determines the partition for a data item using the random function.

While hash and range-based partitioning can result in unbalanced partitions (some partitions having many more data items than others), round-robin results in balanced partitions. But even with round-robin or random partitioning, if tuples can also be removed, it is possible that some partitions may have more data extracted than others. More importantly, hash and range partitioning have an important advantage compared to round-robin and random: it is possible to prune partitions if we are searching based on the value of the partition identifier. It means that only partitions that contain the identifier value need to be searched when queries using that identifier are submitted. For instance, if a query is looking for tuples with the identifier value 10, only partitions containing 10 in the range (range partitioning) or the hash value of 10 that results from applying the defined hash function have to be tested.

Range partitioning also eases the job of searching data items whose identifier is within a certain range, by intersecting the partition ranges with the query ranges. For instance, consider the following statement:

Select * where x between 15 and 25

If the partitions are P1[0,10], P2[11,20], P3[21,30], P4[31,40], then the query will require searching P2 and P3, pruning P1 and P4. If random or round-robin was used, the query would need to search all partitions for data. If hash-partitioning was used and organized into the above partitions based on ranges of hash values, the query processing engine would need to compute the hash of each identifier value from 15 to 25 and consider the corresponding hash-range partitions.

It is possible to define partitions and chunks within partitions. Consider partitioning over a hash-range from 0 to 99. If we have 10 nodes, we can define 10 partitions with ranges 0-9, 10-19, ..., 90-99. Given a chunk size of 100 MB and a dataset size of 100 GB, each partition will be expected to have about 10 GB of data, divided into 100 chunks. If data partitions are unbalanced, for instance, one partition has 18 GB and another one has only 3 GB, then the mapping of hash ranges to partitions can be modified, or the biggest partitions can be split into smaller hash-ranges.

Data can also be partitioned by a combination of more than one attribute. In that case the values (either the values themselves, ranges or hashes) of a set of attributes determine the partitions. For instance, the following are partitions on (brand, month): (brand#1, January 2014), (brand#2, January 2014), (brand#1, February 2014).

Placement is another important concept related to partitioning and to scalability. It refers to the distribution of partitions into nodes in an environment with multiple distinct storage devices, usually in a shared-nothing environment. It concerns how partitions are put into nodes. Both partitioning and placement are very important for scalability in traditional relational data management systems, and whenever big data needs to be joined. The most adequate partitioning can reduce the need to process many partitions, and inadequate placement can result in enormous data exchange overheads between nodes.

Partitioning the data into multiple nodes or cores and processing each in parallel can obtain a considerable speedup. The Partition and Replicate Strategy (PRS) [97][98] proposes partitioning the biggest relation of a schema and replicating all other relations, then processing proceeds in parallel in all nodes. This minimizes network exchange costs for processing joins in a shared-nothing approach, and maximizes the local computation of partial results.

4.2. Partitioning for Data Lifecycle Management

Storing and processing ever-increasing amounts of data may not be the most intelligent way to manage data. This becomes a significant problem when the amounts of data are significant and/or data is added at considerably high rates. It is necessary to define ways to manage old data and/or to organize the data in a way that maintains scalability, in spite of the amounts of data.

If the data is simply added incrementally forever, and the system receives a steady and significant amount of data throughout its lifetime, it becomes difficult to guarantee performance as soon as the data reaches enormous proportions.

Data lifecycle management concerns approaches to reduce the size of the data that needs to be stored and computed upon, by considering data validity. Data validity concerns an amount of time after which data older than that time is considered out of date. In some systems, it might be enough to simply delete data that passed its validity, while in other systems data is archived or summarized. Combinations of these alternatives are also valid in many systems.

Example 1: Consider, as an example, a public transportation ticketing application that sells chargeable transport cards to the public, allows users to charge trips in the card and records every individual ticket validation in metro, city buses, trains and all other types of public transportation. This system needs to compute the division of revenues for each transport operator. Ticket validation devices in each transportation vehicle collect validations, and the data is later forwarded to a central data warehouse where the location, identification of the ticket, timestamp and other information are stored for each validation. If the main table recording every validation receives 500 MB or 1GB of new data every day, it wil soon reach huge sizes. This data will have to be processed and joined with ticket table in a relational database. Computational tasks determining how the revenues from validations should be divided per company will run slower every month as the size of the data increases, until the performance becomes unacceptable.

However, transport cards can have a validity period after which they cannot be charged anymore, and both tickets and validation information that is no longer valid are removed from the main database.

There are two main possible options to keep the size of the data within the appropriate limit of efficiency without erasing or summarizing any data. The first possible solution involves the identification of a range of validity of the data, and past data whose validity period has been exceeded is moved to a twin table with older data. By keeping only information pertaining to the "valid" period in the master repository, efficiency is guaranteed. The limitation of this approach is when it is necessary to query the old data or both, since then we need to redirect queries to the appropriate data set and possibly merge results.

A second solution involves partitioning tables, if the DBMS offers that functionality. Instead of archiving old data, data from the main repository is partitioned into temporal intervals. Queries submitted against the system should specify a time interval, for example the last two years, and the database engine must be able to automatically prune, which consists of accessing only the partitions of the data that correspond to the ranges/hashes of values specified in the query range, thereby saving a significant amount of processing time.

The following example creates a "validations" table, containing ticket validations partitioned by months. The creation statement indicates three partitions for January, February and march. In a DBMS supporting partition pruning, the query indicated after the table creation command should only need to access a single partition of the table, even if the table is extremely big.

```
CREATE TABLE validations
(ticket NUMBER(10),
geo VARCHAR2(30),
timestamp TIMESTAMP)
PARTITION BY RANGE(timestamp)
(
PARTITION            validations_jan2010        VALUES        LESS
THAN(TO_DATE('02/01/2010','DD/MM/YYYY')),
PARTITION            validations_feb2010        VALUES        LESS
THAN(TO_DATE('03/01/2010','DD/MM/YYYY')),
PARTITION            validations_mar2010        VALUES        LESS
THAN(TO_DATE('04/01/2010','DD/MM/YYYY'))
);
```

```
SELECT COUNT(*), geo
FROM validations
WHERE timestamp BETWEEN '01-FEB-2010' AND '28-FEB-2010'
Group by geo;
```

4.3. Workload-based Partitioning

Consider a parallel/distributed system and any database schema. While most relational algebra operations are easily parallelizable over the parallel system, joins are harder to parallelize efficiently, since they must try to match every row of one relation with every row of another relation, outputting the matches. The Partition and Replicate strategy [97][98] (PRS) divides the largest relation and replicates all other relations of the schema, so that joins will still be able to run without considerable exchange of data between nodes.

Whether the objective is for dividing the data among a set of nodes or for accessing only the data that is needed by a query or both, in this section we discuss the more sophisticated principles behind workload-based partitioning.

Remember the multi-dimensional model of a data warehouse and the star schema, which were discussed in Chapter 1 and we illustrate here again in Figure 4.1 and Figure 4.2 for reference.

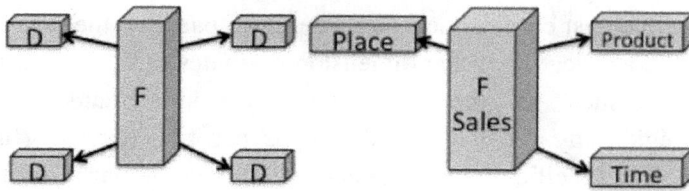

(a) Star Schema(b) Sales Fact

Figure 4.1 – Star Schema

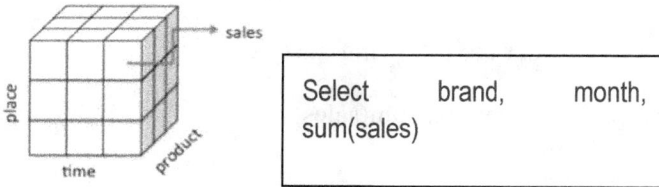

Select   brand,   month, sum(sales)

Figure 4.2 – Multidimensional view and Query

A query workload is a set of queries [Qi]. Imagine a query or group of queries that selects a region of the multidimensional dataset. If the dataset is partitioned such that the required region stays in a single partition, then those queries only need to scan that partition.

This motivates query-workload-based partitioning as described for instance in [62].

A query workload QW([Qi,fi]) is defined as a set of queries [Qi] and the frequency fi with which each query Qi is executed. Each query has aggregations and, most importantly, aggregation grouping attributes, defined as the set of attributes from dimension tables that appear in the group by clause of a query.

Consider a star schema with a large fact table (with many tuples) and much smaller dimensions that fit comfortably in the available memory. Only the fact table is partitioned, and dimensions will reside fully in-memory for faster processing of join operations.

Given a desired number of partitions N, and a query workload with each query specifying query ranges in each dimension, the algorithm should determine the best combination of attributes to partition the dataset. One additional complication is that dimension attributes most frequently form hierarchies, such as year-month-week-day-hour, brand-product or country-region-city-street. If the dataset is partitioned by day and the query needs a specific month, it is enough to read the partitions holding data from all days of that month.

A query Qi is defined as,

Qi[A(expresison),W(expression),GB(expression)]

For instance, consider the following query,

> Select brand, month, sum(sales)
> From [dim(i)], fact
> Where year=2014
> Group by brand, month

The query has group-by attributes brand and month, computes a sum of sales, and constrains the results to the year 2014, therefore it could be summarized as,

> **Q1**[AGGREG(sum(sales)),
> WHERE(year=2014),GB(brand,month)]

A partitioning (key)set PS_i is a set of attributes and their values that determines partitions. For instance, if the partitioning combination is PS(brand,year), then the following are some partitions on (brand, year): (brand#1, 2014), (brand#2, 2014), (brand#1, 2013).

The goal of workload-based partitioning and placement is to find the partitioning keyset PS that will be most efficient for queries. If some queries only need to access some partitions instead of all, then the cost of executing those queries decreases. Given the query workload QW, the partitioning keyset should be one that minimizes the sum of the processing costs for the queries of QW.

To list all possible partitioning keysets for a multi-dimensional dataset, one can consider all combinations of any number of dimensional attributes ($d_i.a_i$) where one dimension appears at most once. It is also possible to restrict the search space to the attributes that appear in the W and GB clauses of queries. The cost of each candidate partitioning keyset is computed as the number of tuples read by each query times the weight of that query in the workload (the weight is given by the frequency with which the query executes). The algorithm is,

For a partitioning keyset PSi,

$$\text{cost}_{PSi} = \text{WEIGHETED}$$
$$\text{SUM}_{\text{all queries } Qi}(\text{number of tuples read from all partitions}$$
$$\text{that need to be accessed by the query Qi})$$

The PS_i with lowest cost cost_{PSi} is chosen. Since there should also be a limit on the number of partitions, the solutions can alternatively be the PS_i with lowest cost cost_{PSi} that results in a number of partitions within a tolerance factor from the target number of partitions.

In a parallel DBMS the query processor parallelizes execution by processing partitions in a divided fashion over the processing units. On-demand processing should be used, whereby processing units ask for more work when they finished processing a partition. If the parallel architecture is shared-nothing, the partitions should be placed into nodes following an approach similar to the one we delineated in Chapter 3 for on-demand chunk processing. Finally, it is also possible to work with partitions and fixed-size chunks within the partitions.

4.4. Workload-Join Partition&Place (P&P)

While a simple star schema where every dimension is small can easily be partitioned in a parallel setup using the Partition and Replicate strategy [97][98] (PRS), resulting in each node having approximately 1/n of the data, and a considerable speedup can be expected, the transformation shown in Figure 4.3 represents a more difficult scenario. The example is a representation of the TPC-H schema [24], where the tables are (P-part, S-supplier, PS-partsupp, LI-Lineitem, O-orders, C-customer) and the table sizes are represented relatively to each other. The objective is still to place partitions into nodes for parallel data processing. However, in these schemas there are multiple tables with significant sizes. Since, in order to achieve a significant speedup, every node in an n nodes setup should have to process only about 1/n of the data, every relation that is significant in terms of size should be partitioned and the partitions should be divided into the nodes, and only small relations can be replicated. This is a necessary condition to achieve a speedup similar to the number of nodes/processing units of the parallel architecture. But it is not a sufficient condition. The partitioning in Figure 4.3 has some subtle implications regarding the processing of joins, as we will discuss next. Another issue is what should be considered small and what should be considered significant in terms of size. Processing costs end up reflecting in execution times, therefore a small table size is one that has low impact in total execution time of the query if the table is replicated into all nodes instead of partitioned.

The independent execution of partial joins by nodes is possible in PRS [97][98] because all except one of the relations in the star (that is, all dimensions) are replicated into all nodes. Considering a fully-partitioned relation Ri and all the remaining ones replicated into all nodes, the relevant join property is:

$$R_1 \bowtie D_2 \bowtie \ldots \bowtie D_i \bowtie \ldots D_n = \bigcup_{j=1}^{all\_nodes} R_1 \bowtie D_2 \bowtie \ldots D_i \bowtie \ldots D_n \quad (1)$$

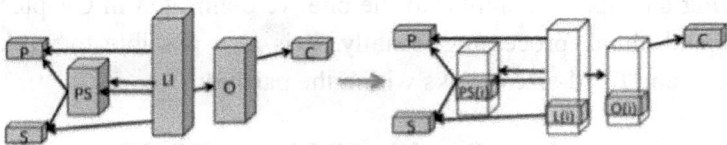

Figure 4.3 – Partitioning a Complex Schema

Consider now the case of a query joining tables LI-O-PS-P-S in Figure 4.3. Since a join is a match between rows with the same join-key value in two relations, the join when executed in a parallel architecture can only be executed without any data shipment between nodes if the partitions of the two relations in each node correspond to the same join key value ranges. And this is not even feasible in the case of joining more than two partitioned relations as in the example LI-O-PS-P-S. It is possible to equi-partition two of the relations (partition by the join attribute and place accordingly in nodes), but then a third partitioned relation will not be equi-partitioned. For instance, if relations Lineitem (LI) and Orders (O) are both partitioned by the join key (orderkey) and placed into the nodes such that orderkey values in each node match, then LI will not be equi-partitioned with Partsupplier (PS), since the join key is different. Joining non-equi-partitioned relations requires on-the-fly repartitioning (to match keys in each node), which is very costly in shared-nothing architecture due to data exchanges.

More generically, given three relations R1, R2 and R3 where R1 and R2 are equi-partitioned and R3 is partitioned but the key is different, then joining with R3 will be potentially costly. Either R3 partitions are shipped into all nodes to reconstruct R3 for the join, or the intermediate result of joining R1 and R2 will have to be re-hashed to the partitioning identifier that will join with R3. The query performance is going to suffer from considerable overhead, and perhaps it would be better to simply keep relation R3 replicated into all nodes from the start. It is the job of the query optimizer to determine the best execution plan, but the data placement partitioning choices impact the alternatives.

$$ R_1 \bowtie R_2 \bowtie R_3 = \bigcup_{j=1}^{all\_nodes} (R_{1j} \bowtie R_{2j} \bowtie R_3) \qquad (5) $$

In what concerns alternative parallel join processing algorithms, the following lists the alternatives. A cost-based query optimizer must estimate the cost of using each alternative based on statistics and choose the least costly one for each join in each alternative complex query plan that needs to be evaluated to determine the best plan for execution of a query:

- Replicated Join: if only one table is partitioned and all remaining tables are completely replicated into all nodes, the join can occur in parallel with no data exchange requirements between nodes;
- Co-located or equi-partitioned join: the data is already partitioned according to the join hash values, so the join can occur in parallel with no data exchange requirements between nodes;

- Redirected join: the data is not co-located but it is enough to re-locate the rows from one of the source data sets in order to co-locate them and proceed with a co-located join;
- Repartitioned join: both source data sets need to be re-located in order to become co-located;
- Broadcast join: one of the source data is broadcasted into all nodes to enable parallel joining with the other partitioned data set.

Workload-Join partitioning and placement is an approach to determine the most appropriate partitioning attributes for placement of data in a shared-nothing environment, to optimize processing of joins. The objective is to minimize the costs of repartitioning, which are incurred when two relations that have to be joined are not equi-partitioned (hash-partitioned into nodes by the join key). Then, there is a rehash and shipment of data to nodes, so that in the end they will be equi-partitioned (partitioned by the join key). Considering large relations with size Ti, N nodes and a simple linear cost model, the data size of partitioned relations per node is Ti/N. β is a partitioning cost weight and α a local processing cost weight, so that β/α denotes the ratio of partitioning cost to local processing cost. The join-processing cost for queries requiring the join between equi-partitioned large relations and including also small relations ri is:

Cost with equi-partitioned tables T1 and T2 and small tables ti =

$$\alpha \times \left(\frac{T_1}{N} + \frac{T_2}{N} + t_1 + \dots + t_l \right) \qquad (6)$$

The cost when large relations are not equi-partitioned on a switched network includes repartitioning and local processing cost factors with corresponding weights, as shown in (4). The IR symbol represents the size of intermediate results from processing local parts of queries (those that do not require data exchange between nodes). The value IR/N is the fraction of the IR that is at each node. About 1/N of that fraction (1/N x IR/N) has the correct hash-value for the node, therefore requires no repartitioning. The cost of repartitioned join involves the cost of repartitioning the intermediate results and the cost of processing locally.

Cost of repartitioning T1 and T2 for join processing =

$$\left(\frac{IR}{N} - \frac{IR}{N^2}\right) \times \beta + \alpha \times \left(\frac{T_1}{N} + \frac{T_2}{N} + t_1 + ... + t_l\right) \qquad (7)$$

The increase in cost is therefore $\left(\frac{IR}{N} - \frac{IR}{N^2}\right) \times \beta$.

The Workload-Join partitioning and placement algorithm is based in the concept of join links (linking every two relations that are joined in the query workload), and adding a cost to each link, which represents the cost of repartitioning the relations involved in that join. A repartitioning cost of query Qi is given by the cost of re-hashing (with shipment) the intermediate result sets that result from processing part of the query locally in each node. A query has selection conditions over table tuples and joins with small replicated tables, all of which can be done locally. The resulting intermediate results IR are then repartitioned according to the join attribute that is going to be used in the next join. In the example of Figure 4.4 there are three queries (Q1, Q2, Q3), each requiring joins of partitioned tables, and each of those queries is assumed to occur a number of times in the workload. The corresponding graph is shown in the right of the figure.

Given this graph, the algorithm to pick the most adequate equi-partitioning attributes is,

For each relation R
      Pick the link with highest cost containing the relation
      The relation R is to be partitioned by the links' equi-join attribute;

            IR= size of intermediate result
            Q1 (R1,R2), freq 8
            Q2 (R2,R4), freq 2
            Q3 (R3,R4), freq 4

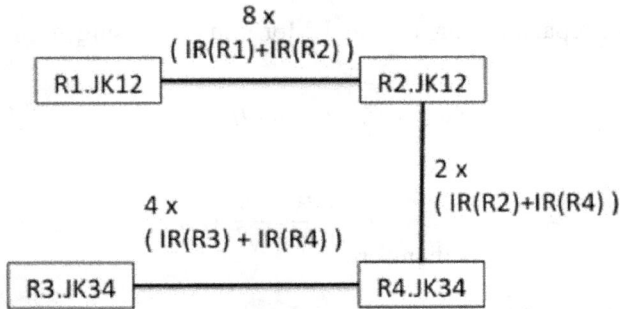

Figure 4.4 – Workload-Join Costs

4.5. Use of Workload-based Partitioning

Figure 4.5 illustrates the steps involved in partitioning the data according to the workload, and Figure 4.7 illustrates the steps involved in processing the partitioned data. The tables represented in Figure 4.5 are those of TPC–H (P=part, S=supplier, PS=partsupp, LI=lineorder, O=orders, C=customer). The WKLOAD algorithm determines the appropriate partitioning based on the algorithm we described in this chapter, resulting in the partitioned tables illustrated in the same figure. Those tables are then placed (or re-organized) according to that result in a set of parallel processing nodes.

The second step, illustrated in Figure 4.6, refers to query processing. A COST-based optimizer must decide which operations to do in which order (execution plan) over the whole set of parallel nodes. As much as possible of the processing is done in parallel over all nodes simultaneously. This includes early selections, joins over equi-partitioned tables and joins of replicated tables to individual partitioned tables or intermediate results. Since there can be non-equi-partitioned tables, a data repartitioning step may be required, followed by additional parallel processing over all nodes. For instance, Figure 4.6 shows two alternatives, where replicated dimension tables can be joined in parallel with one or the other of non-equi-partitioned fact tables, before being repartitioned and continuing the query processing.

4.6. Co-located Partitioning for Dependent Relations

By taking into consideration workloads and workload frequencies, workload-based and workload-join based partitioning are optimized ways to determine partitioning. However, we can also use some simple heuristics to decide partitioning manually. For instance, in TPC-H the relation LineItem contains lineitems from the relation Orders.

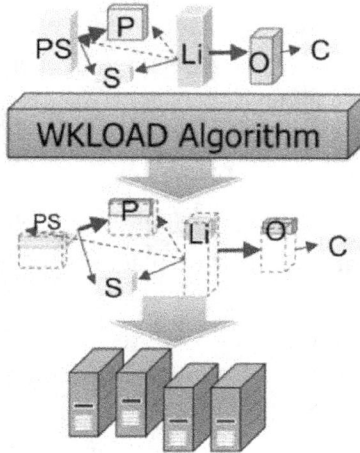

Figure 4.5 –Step 1: Partitioning and Placing (TPC-H)

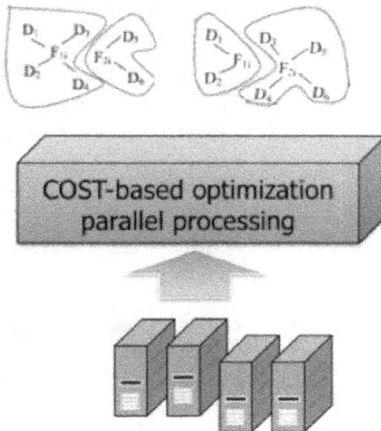

Figure 4.6 –Step 2: Processing Partitioned Data (TPC-H)

If we co-locate every lineitem with the corresponding Order, then we will be able to join both relations in individual partitions independently from the other partitions. Lineitem is called the dependent relation in a many-one relationship with Orders, and Orders is called the principal. A simple heuristic for manual decisions is to replicate every small relation that fits comfortably in memory into all nodes (partitions), then try to co-locate dependent relations when the principal relation needs to be partitioned, while the principal relation can be partitioned randomly or round-robin. Of course the database engine query processor must be aware of the partitioning choices.

4.7. Brief Experimental Analysis

Next, we briefly analyze experimentally the performance without and with workload-join partitioning and placement (P&P). The setup uses TPC-H benchmark [68] with a scale factor of 100GB installed on an Oracle DBMS and running in 25 PCs (Windows XP, with 2GB RAM, 200 GB disks and Ultra-ATA). After running the Workload-Join partitioning and placement algorithm (WKJ-B), the resulting partitioning is shown in Figure 4.7, where the partitioning attributes are shown, as well as the following notation: dashed arrowed links represent the need to repartition, thick arrowed links represent equi-partitioned datasets, and thin arrowed links represent replicated joins (with small dimensions).

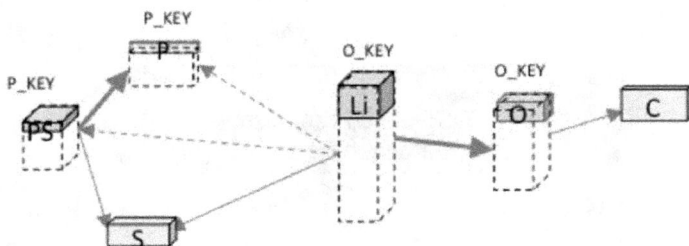

Figure 4.7 – WKJB Partitioning Result (TPC-H)

This partitioning and placement WKJB is compared with the alternative, called Partition and Replicate (PRS), of partitioning the largest LI relation and replicating all the remaining ones, to avoid repartitioning costs. Figure 4.8 shows the results. In that figure it is clear that the Workload-Join Partitioning algorithm (WKJB) was able to achieve speedups on the order of the degree of parallelism (25 nodes). Some speedups are super-linear (above the degree of parallelism), which is due to a move from I/O to memory when datasets fit into memory. In what concerns some low speedups of the Partition and Replicate approach (PRS), a closer look at the queries form TPC-H reveals that those correspond to queries that access very large relations that were not partitioned, in particular the Orders table. The conclusion form this experiment is that it is worth applying the WKJB algorithm when schemas are more complex than simple star schemas with small dimensions and large fact tables.

4.8. Further Reading

Issues related with implementing data management systems over conventional shared-nothing architectures are reviewed in [15, 21, 103]. They include partitioning, processing, replication and load-balancing. One of the first works reviewing partitioning and concluding that it has considerable effect on performance was [91]. Variable partitioning was proposed in [31] (size and access frequency-based). DWPA [18, 19, 20] uses workload-partitioning, partitioning large relations and copying smaller ones to optimize processing. Hash-partitioning of relations minimizes costs of parallel join processing [42]. Parallel hash-join algorithms are reviewed in [76].

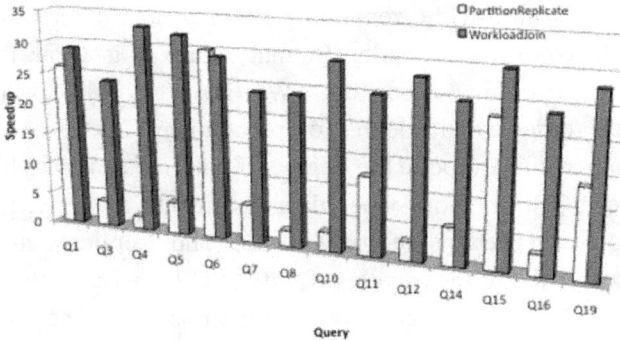

Figure 4.8 – Speedup on 25 Nodes (relative to 1 node)

The following two references proposed approaches to search for the best hash-partitions that maximize equi-hash joins on shared-nothing nodes [57, 76]. Attribute-wise derived partitioning was proposed in [63] and [4]. [63] included join-bitmap indexes together with attribute-wise derived partitioning and hierarchy-aware processing.

The works in [97][98] discussed and tested a Partition and Replicate approach for distributed query processing. [104] proposes replicating all dimensions and partitioning facts in star schemas. The approach in [95] shows how to achieve efficient allocation of multi-dimensional databases based on the workload, and [96]also investigates partitioning in data warehouses and data marts. References [22] and [23] explore on-demand load-balancing and chunk-based partition and replicate approaches to optimize processing of multi-dimensional data sets.

Older references on partitioning approaches include [99] and [100].

5. Concurrent Workloads

Traditional database management systems have been designed to handle concurrently submitted queries independently of each other (the query-at-a-time execution model) [12]. Each submitted query determines an execution plan, which is then followed from start to end, until the query is completely processed. One of the problems of this model is that it does not scale well to an environment with many queries running concurrent and unpredictable workloads. If the size of datasets is significant and heavy operations exist (e.g. heavy joins), the amount of processing and resources that are necessary for processing even a single query can already be significant. But, when there are multiple simultaneous queries, the number of queries/sessions running simultaneously multiplies the amount of processing and resources that are consumed. The system lacks scalability to concurrent query workloads. This problem is independent of whether it runs on a single server or a parallel server system. In this chapter we describe the generic approach that can be used to provide scalability in the presence of multiple concurrent queries. Spin [12] proposes I/O and processing sharing over a denormalized star schema. Other works have proposed slightly different approaches [26, 69, 78, 79, 81, 90]. This kind of approaches are also related to dataflow architectures in general (data flows (data push) to and between processing operators, instead of query processors retrieving the data (data pull). In this chapter we discuss I/O and processing sharing generically, considering star schemas.

5.1. Handling Concurrent Workloads

If we can share processing of several queries instead of processing each query separately, the system becomes scalable to concurrent queries. Therefore, the solution is based in creating a shared query-processing pipelined tree through which data is transformed to fit queries requirements, with as much sharing as possible by all queries. However, there are some issues that must be solved for this to work. For instance, queries may share part of the processing, however they are submitted at different time instants, so there must be a way for later queries to process all the data as well. Another problem is that join operations are usually not implemented as simple transformations over a stream of data that would fit easily into the pipelined processing tree.

Considering that a typical data warehouse schema is made of a set of star schemas, with typically big central fact tables and a set of dimension tables pointed by foreign keys of the fact table, we assume that dimensions are kept in-memory and fact tables do not fit in memory. Queries submitted to the star schema usually have a lot of common processing tasks, in particular those related to scanning the fact table and joining with dimensions. Those operations represent most of the total query processing cost.

Scalability can be achieved by modifying the query processor to have three main mechanisms: On one hand, tables that fit comfortably into memory are pre-loaded. Dimensions are hash-organized into memory, so that joins between the fact table and dimensions are transformed into fast hash lookups; I/O scanning of fact tables, which become the most expensive operation, are shared by all queries. Fact rows read in those scans are fed into query processing pipelines. Finally, the queries themselves share as much as possible of the query execution plan, besides the low-level I/O. For instance, if two queries access the same table and filter the results by the same attribute value, then it is only necessary to do so once and share the resulting rows for the two queries.

5.2. Cyclic Query Processing

Figure 5.1 shows how the simple primitive operations of Scan and Join can be organized to optimize the processing of multiple query sessions concurrently. When a query arrives, a bitmap is created per dimension for matching the dimension with the query predicates. The bitmap distinguishes dimension rows that are included by the predicate to those that are excluded. This approach allows faster evaluation of the join between the fact and dimensions. The (disk-based) fact table is fully scanned sequentially and repeatedly while there are queries being processed. Tuples are brought into memory and, for each query, the join of the tuple with each dimension is evaluated.

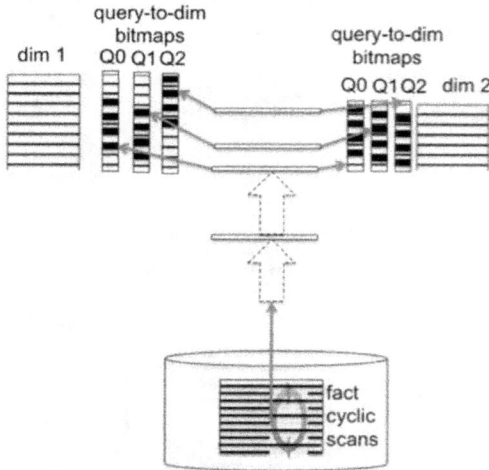

Figure 5.1 – Cyclic scans and in-memory bitmap-based join

Figure 5.2 shows how new queries are accommodated in the design. The scanning of fact tables is always running (spinning), as long as there are queries requiring more tuples. When the scan arrives at the end of the scanning of the fact, it continues scanning from the first fact row, only stopping when there are no queries to be served (all queries already processed all fact rows). When a query is submitted, it is "registered" to start processing fact tuples, and it will receive fact tuples until a complete scan of all the tuples of the fact is done for the query. For instance, in Figure 5.2, query Q0 was the first to be submitted. Scanning of the fact table started at that moment, in position 0 of the fact table. When the scan was in position p1, a new query arrived – query Q1, and when it was in position p2, another query was submitted (Q2). While query Q0 ended its processing after the fact was scanned once (because it processed all fact tuples), the fact will be scanned again from position 0 to feed the data remaining for queries Q1 and Q2. Q1 will end its processing after the second scan arrives at p1, and Q2 will end its processing when the scan arrives at p2.

This mechanism shares scanning of fact tuples into all queries that are actively running, since tuples are "pushed" into queries. This mechanism together with in-memory lookups and query-dimension bitmaps makes the approach scale to large concurrent workloads, in contrast to the traditional query processor that scan and process independently for each query. The circular loop is continuously spinning, sequentially reading data chunks while there are queries running.

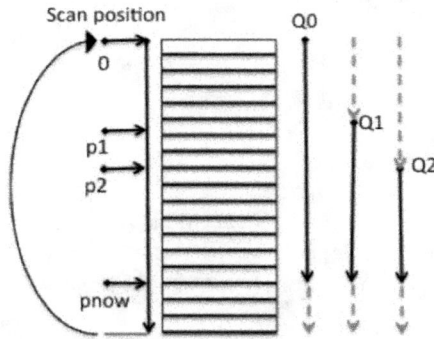

Figure 5.2 – Spinning the Scans over Queries

5.3. Operators Sharing

Sharing of processing steps is another important part of handling concurrent workloads efficiently. For instance, Spin [12] defines a query processing pipeline and a workload processing tree that shares operators between queries as much as possible.

Operator sharing approaches are usually based in representing queries as pipelines of operators, then sharing the common prefixes of those pipelines. Consider the following set of operators:

Θ_F – scan fact F
$Y_{x,y}$ – aggregation grouping by attributes x,y
$\sigma_{predicate\ x}$ – selection predicate x
Π – projection operator

The following query expressed here in SQL is then represented in (relational) operators notation using the symbols defined above.

Select sum(sales), year, brand
From sales JOIN time JOIN product
Where year>=2000
Group by year, brand;

$\Pi_{sum(sales),\ year,\ brand}\ (Y_{year,brand}\ (\sigma_{year>=2000}\ (\Theta_{sales})\ )\ )$

In this representation we do not include JOINS as operators. This corresponds to assuming the logic multidimensional dataset (cube) instead of the relational implementation. In practice, joins are processed using the simple in-memory lookup procedure that we described before and are not included in the notation.

The operators are executed in the following order:

$(\Theta_{sales})\ \text{->}\ (\sigma_{year>=2000})\ \text{->}\ (Y_{year,brand})\ \text{->}\ (\Pi_{sum(sales),\ year,\ brand})$

Consider that the following query is also submitted:

Select sum(sales), year, brand
From sales JOIN time JOIN product
Where year>=2001 and City='Coimbra'
Group by year, brand;

$\Pi_{sum(sales),\ year,\ brand}\ (Y_{year,brand}\ (\sigma_{year>=2001\ and\ City='Coimbra'}\ (\Theta_{sales})\ )\ )$

The selection operator of this query can be rewritten to include the selection operator of the previous query as early-filtering:

$$\sigma_{\text{year>=2001 and City='Coimbra'}} \Rightarrow (\sigma_{\text{year>=2000}}) \rightarrow (\sigma_{\text{year>=2001 and City='Coimbra'}})$$

The shared operator processing pipeline is shown next. In that pipeline sales tuples are scanned and retrieved first to feed the pipeline. The common filter (year>=2000) is processed next and then the pipeline branches into two independent processing pipelines, one for each of the two queries.

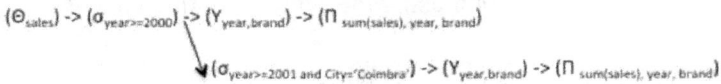

$$(\Theta_{\text{sales}}) \rightarrow (\sigma_{\text{year>=2000}}) \rightarrow (Y_{\text{year,brand}}) \rightarrow (\Pi_{\text{sum(sales), year, brand}})$$

$$\downarrow (\sigma_{\text{year>=2001 and City='Coimbra'}}) \rightarrow (Y_{\text{year,brand}}) \rightarrow (\Pi_{\text{sum(sales), year, brand}})$$

Figure 5.3 shows an example pipeline that would be derived by Spin [12] for feeding three queries that are running simultaneously. Spin includes a Data Switch component to route tuples into branches [12]. The query formulation can be reconstructed from the pipeline:

- Query Q0 = select sum($\in$), country from X where year>2010 and brand!='A' group by country having sum($\in$)> 2M
- Query Q1 = select sum($\in$), country from X where year>2010 and brand!='A' group by country
- Query Q2 = select sum($\in$), country from X where year>2010 and city='London' group by street

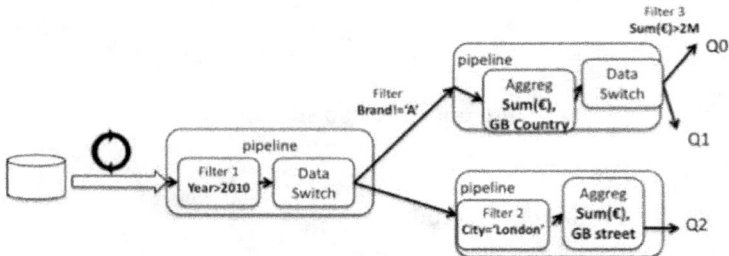

Figure 5.3 –Data Processing Pipeline example

This pipeline has to be updated automatically. Spin [12] defines how these pipelines are built and reorganized each time a new query is submitted or ends processing.

6. Realtime Scalable Data Warehouse

Realtime warehouses are data warehouses that integrate new data with a small latency from the instant when the event that generated that data occurred in the data source / operational system. A scalable realtime data warehouse system should be able to integrate data as quickly as desired, regardless of the data ingress rate and the size of the data warehouse. In this chapter we analyse how to achieve realtime and scalable realtime integration in data warehouse systems. This problem has also been the focus of many other works, including [16, 39, 52, 75, 77].

6.1. RealTime Data Warehouses

As described in chapter 1, the data to be integrated into a data warehouse is extracted periodically or in realtime from data sources, using what is called the Extract-Transform-Load (ETL) workflow.

Data sources provide input for periodic data extraction. The term realtime refers to integrating new data and making it available for analysis as soon as it is generated, with a minimum latency. For extraction, the system needs to have a way to know the update set, representing the new data entered and modified in the data sources since the last extraction happened. Change Data Capture (CDC) mechanisms [56, 61, 39, 75] are a common way to do that efficiently over an operational data system.

The extracted data then goes into a staging area, the place where transformation and loading happens. Transformation refers to the modifications that data goes through for conforming to the warehouse schema. Loading concerns taking the transformed data and loading it into the data warehouse schemas. Remember that a typical data warehouse has several star schemas, materialized views (summary tables) and indexes, which are used for faster access to specific query patterns. The loading and refreshing of all those structures can be a time-consuming job. Loading can be significantly delayed for at least two main reasons: if indexes, constraints and other auxiliary structures are kept during the loading process, then there will be a slowdown of the process, since updating those structures takes time and must be done for each row that is inserted/modified/deleted; loading is also severely slowed when running simultaneously with query sessions being submitted and processed by the system; Conversely, query response times can be increased during online loading.

The process of refreshing redundant structures such as materialized views also competes for the same resources as query processing, and increases loading plus refreshing times.

The final step that we should consider is analyzing, querying, reporting and mining the data warehouse. In order for a data warehouse to be realtime, it is also important to provide almost interactive answers to queries. Loading, refreshing and querying are critical processes in a realtime warehouse.

Figure 6.1 shows the traditional data warehouse architecture, while Figure 6.2 shows the components that may need to be added to make it realtime. Notice that a realtime component was added to the data warehouse, the RT-DW component. Next we will describe each part that was modified to achieve realtime functionality.

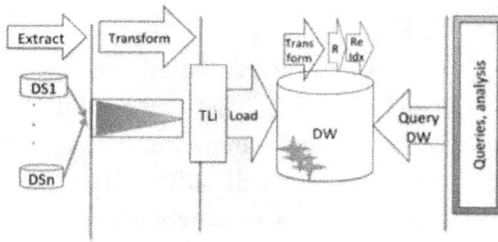

Figure 6.1 – Traditional warehousing components

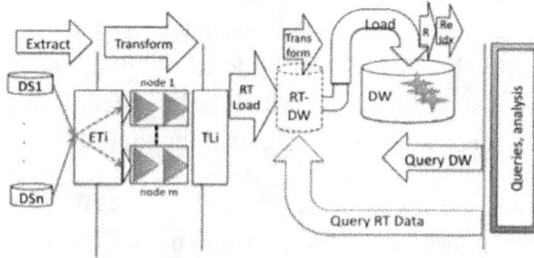

Figure 6.2 – Realtime warehousing components

6.2. Data Transformation

Transformations can be seen as a set of operations occurring in sequence. Transformation scalability, for handling high-rate data, can be obtained using both pipelining and partitioning, as shown in Figure 6.2. Pipelining involves specifying transformation as a sequence of specific transform operations, each feeding the next one. Individual operations can be processed in different cores or nodes in a cluster. Transformation can also be parallelized. The data to be processed is partitioned into different processor units, and processed in parallel. Each tuple of data coming from data sources, or each set of tuples of data is assigned to a different processing unit. If each processing unit has its own data structures, such as lookup tables, then those processing units can process incoming tuples in parallel.

6.3. Loading and Querying

Realtime loading can be achieved based on the added realtime component, RT-DW in Figure 6.2. That component should reside in a different node from the main data warehouse. It has essentially the same base data warehouse schema, but will only contain the recent data that was not yet loaded into the main data warehouse, and it does not contain any auxiliary structures (indexes, materialized views). For instance, if the data is loaded once a day, the RT-DW will contain only data from the current day. Real-time loading is done on that component, while the main data warehouse is always online, answering queries and not being loaded simultaneously. The use of the RT-DW component shifts loading of new data into that component, which is less loaded in terms of query processing since it has much less data than the main DW.

Queries accessing the recent data go to the RT-DW component, while queries accessing non-recent data go to the main DW. Queries accessing both recent and old data need to run on both and it is necessary to add a merging component that will merge the results from both parts and provide the final answers.

The following example illustrates the processing of a query that needs access to both parts of the data warehouse (the main data warehouse and the RT-DW). The original query is rewritten into a query that will run on the RT-DW, a similar query that will run on the normal data warehouse, and a merge query that will merge the results from both parts. Of course, if the query only needs recent data resident in the RT-DW component or older data from the main DW, querying the other part and the merge will not be necessary.

The recent data residing in the RT-DW component still needs to be loaded into the main data warehouse periodically. The traditional mechanism to load data into a data warehouse is offline loading. The data warehouse stops responding to user queries and loads the data.

Original query:
```
select sum(l_revenue), d_year, p_type
from lineorder, date, part, supplier
where
l_orderdate = d_datekey and
l_partkey = p_partkey and
l_suppkey = s_suppkey and
p_type = 'A' and
s_region = 'North'
group by d_year, p_type
order by d_year, p_type;
```

Same modified query runs on data warehouse and realtime component:
```
select l_revenue, d_year, p_type
from lineorder, date, part, supplier
where
l_orderdate = d_datekey and
l_partkey = p_partkey and
l_suppkey = s_suppkey and
p_type = 'A' and
s_region = 'North'
group by d_year, p_type
order by d_year, p_type;
```

In-memory merge query:
```
select sum(l_revenue), d_year, p_type
from (
select l_revenue, d_year, p_type
from resultOfMainDataWarehouse
UNION ALL
   select l_revenue, d_year, p_type
from resultOfRT-DW
)
group by d_year, p_type
order by d_year, p_type;
```

Figure 6.3 – Query re-writing example, process and merge

This can be done during night-time or weekend, to avoid disturbing query processing. The realtime data warehouse allows almost instant integration of new data, but there is still the need to integrate data offline, therefore also to find a dead period in which it is possible to do that.

If 24/7 availability is required as well, there needs to be a stand-by data warehouse. While the main data warehouse is being loaded, the standby data warehouse answers queries. Then the main data warehouse is put online and the standby data warehouse is updated.

6.4. Total Scalability

Parallelization of warehouse nodes also increases the maximum data integration rate that can be achieved and decreases query response times. This is done using the partitioning and query parallelization approaches described in previous chapters. The RT-DW component can also be parallelized for increased data integration rate if necessary. As a coarse simplification, if a RT-DW data warehouse is only capable of loading a maximum of n rows per second, and a maximum rate of n' rows per second should be supported, then there should be $\lceil n'/n \rceil$ nodes to meet that requirement. Figure 6.4 shows an illustration of a data warehouse with all components parallelized.

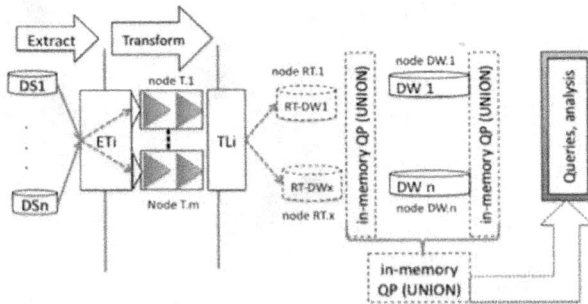

Figure 6.4 – Realtime scalability with parallel warehouse

6.5. Query Results Merging Details

We have discussed the use of a realtime component for implementing realtime data warehouses. Queries submitted to the data warehouse need to be rewritten into a component that should be executed against the RT-DW component and one that should be executed against the main data warehouse. Then the two are merged in a merge component. The need to merge partial results may cause some extra overhead in response time, when compared with the time taken to answer the query over a data warehouse without the RT-DW component. However, the query running against the RT-DW component responds fast even while loading new data, since this component holds only a small fraction of the whole data (the most recent data). This means that the realtime component has the results ready while the larger data warehouse is still processing the query. Merging is also a very efficient process if ran on an in-memory database. In practice, there is a set of alternatives concerning processing and merging:

Processing and merging in a single location, as illustrated in Figure 6.5 considers co-locating both data warehouse components together in a single database. Queries are automatically rewritten into two queries that select data from each of the data warehouse components, joining results using a UNION ALL clause. Since both components co-exist in the same database, there is no need to ship data (partial results) from one component to the other one.

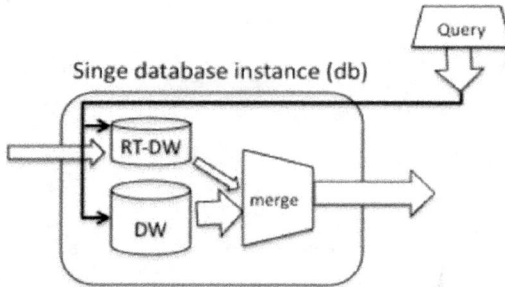

Figure 6.5 – Process and merge in single location

The advantage of the approach is that there is no need to ship partial results between the place where the query is executed and the merge site, since those are the same. But this single-location approach is only possible if the realtime component lives in the same server as the main DW. The problem with this approach is that the realtime component, which was created to avoid loading data directly to the main data warehouse, is now co-located with the main dfata warehouse, which means that the extra overhead of loading impacts the simultaneous processing of queries in the main data warehouse.

If, on the other hand, the realtime data warehouse component is placed in a different machine from the original data warehouse, simultaneity of realtime loading and query processing is avoided over the main data warehouse component. The results from the query ran against the realtime component are shipped into the main data warehouse, where the partial query results are merged with the results from execution against the main data warehouse. This is shown in Figure 6.6. Insertion into the main data warehouse can be done by bulk load, one-by-one or using small batches (e.g jdbc inserts). After the results are integrated into the main DW, a join is executed to merge both partial results and compute the final merged result.

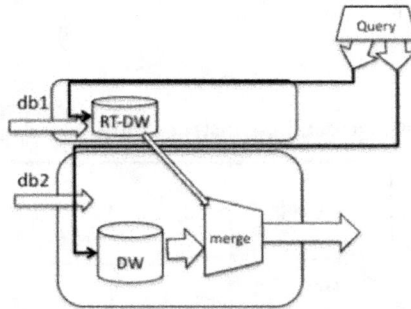

Figure 6.6 –Independent-location with result shipment

The last approach is the fully-independent approach. It keeps the realtime and data warehouse separate, and the merge component also in an independent location, with both data warehouse and realtime components shipping their results to that component. Computed results are migrated to an in-memory database that computes the final results by submitting a merge query. Figure 6.7 illustrates the approach. This approach achieves the best performance, since merging is very fast and there is no mixing of processing of the realtime component with the processing in the main data warehouse and in the merger component.

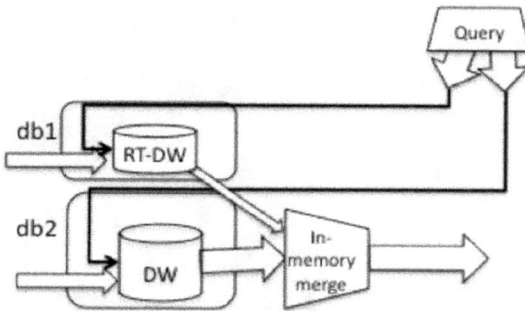

Figure 6.7 – Fully independent processing and merge

6.6. Conclusions and Further References

With the generic mechanisms described in this chapter, it is possible to design a successful realtime data warehouse. There is also experimental evidence to support the relevance of these findings. The authors of [17] have analysed the limitations of traditional data warehouses when trying to achieve near-realtime functionality, that is, when trying to integrate data in near-realtime. They have shown that it is not possible to have realtime in a traditional design, mostly because it is not possible to load data run queries simultaneously while maintaining good performance for both. In [16] the authors analysed the use of a realtime component experimentally, concluding that both loading and querying are no longer impacted negatively when using both components. Finally, they compared experimentally the alternative merge approaches, concluding that keeping all the processing (data warehouse and realtime components) and merge in the same component results in bad performance, and that the fully independent processing and merge approach is able to guarantee the best performance of the three alternatives. Besides these, other related works proposing realtime solutions include [6, 39, 52, 66, 71, 73, 75, 77, 101].

7. Modern Scalability Frameworks

The engineers at Google had to deal with huge datasets and complex computations over those datasets. Their search engine indexes billions of web pages, and very demanding computations over huge amounts of data are necessary in their infrastructure. To meet those demands, Google has more than two hundred clusters of thousands of machines. Developers dealt with those large-scale computations and enormous scalability requirements by designing a platform for internet-scale computations. Google's distributed infrastructure is based on Google File System (GFS), MapReduce and BigTable.

The Google File System (GFS) offers reliable and scalable storage. It is a large distributed log structured file system. GFS provides efficient distribution of data and operations over nodes to minimize bottlenecks. It offers high reliability, scales to thousands of nodes, is capable of offering a very large read and write bandwidth, and supports large blocks of data. Master servers keep file metadata, and the data itself is stored in chunks of 64 MB over the file system. Clients retrieve data by querying the master server, which locates the appropriate chunks, after which clients retrieve the data directly from chunk servers. For fault-tolerance reasons, chunks are replicated over three chunk servers.

While the Google framework is not public, the Apache Hadoop project develops a similar but open-source software framework for reliable, scalable, distributed computing. Figure 7.1 shows the elements of the two stacks, Hadoop and Google. As can be seen from the figure, the "Hadoop Distributed File System" (HDFS) corresponds to the "Google File System" (GFS), as the underlying fault-tolerant and highly-efficient distributed file system. MapReduce is implemented on top of both file systems, for development and operation of highly parallel computations. BigTable and HBase are highly efficient distributed storage systems that work on top of GFS and HDFS respectively. There are many more components, some of them intrinsically part of the framework, others added for increased functionality. ZooKeeper and Chubby are services that allow distributed processes to coordinate with each other and implement functionalities such as distributed lock management (DLM), which allow those distributed processes to synchronize their accesses to shared resources.

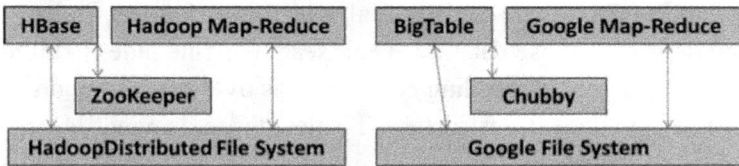

Figure 7.1 – Google and Hadoop Stacks

From the perspective of the user, Hadoop presents a single large storage space. The user sees a single large filesystem and stores data in files. In practice, that storage space is distributed, made of the set of all individual storage spaces of the nodes participating in the cluster. An HDFS cluster has a master server that manages the file system and access to files by clients. Each node in the cluster has one DataNode managing the storage of that node (Datanodes serve read and write requests that were directed by the master server to that node). Internally, a file stored in HDFS is split into blocks that are stored in the DataNodes. The NameNode manages the mapping of blocks to DataNodes. DataNodes also create, delete and replicate blocks when requested by the NameNode.

7.1. MapReduce

Given a set of commodity machines running Hadoop, MapReduce is a software infrastructure for processing parallelizable computations on data across huge datasets using those machines. MapReduce is able to process data stored either on the filesystem or in a database. It requires programmers and other applications using it to convert problems into one of more iterations of the two phases (map and reduce):

Map(): During the map phase, the master server reads the input data from files or database, divides that data into smaller datasets and distributes those datasets to worker nodes. The worker node executes a user-defined map function over each row of the dataset that it received for processing, and writes the output, passing it back to the server node.

Reduce(): The Reduce phase concerns collecting all the outputs from all workers and combining them using the user-defined reduce function into some output.

The map is executed in parallel over the machines participating in the computation, each node taking care of a fraction of the dataset. Similarly, the reduce also executes in parallel, one reducer per node. The map function outputs key-value pairs, and a re-shuffle operation that is executed automatically by MapReduce will redistribute the output data into reducers, such that a specific key value goes to a specific reducer.

Since MapReduce can run over a large set of computers to process enormous datasets, it is important to tolerate failures. If a map or reduce job fails, MapReduce re-schedules the corresponding computation just for the failed jobs.

The input data to MapReduce is structured as (key,value) pairs, where the key is an identifier attribute and the value is the rest of the data item or tuple. Map receives the (key,value) pairs in parallel in all nodes processing map jobs, lets say (k1,v1). Map then does in every node whatever was coded for the processing of the row, and writes to the output another (key,value) pair that it produces from the tuple, say (k2,v2). The output of the map function is therefore a set of (key,value) pairs as well. That output is organized into files in each node, such that each file has the set of tuples with the same key value. The MapReduce software redistributes (key, value) outputs that resulted from the map function and "groups them" based on the value of the key. Each key value is assigned to a reducer, and reducers run in parallel over all nodes participating in the reduction phase. The logical input to the reducer is therefore a pair (k3, set of values with key k3). The output of the reduce function can be for instance some merging operation (e.g. the sum of all values with key k3 or the number of tuples with value k3). The final result is the collection of all results from all reducers.

The following is a frequently given example that illustrates programming map and reduce functions. The objective is to count the occurrences of individual words in a set of documents [50]:

```
function map(String documentName, String document):
for each word w in document:
   emitIntermediate (w, 1)

function reduce(String word, Iterator listOfOccurences):
sum = 0
 for each occur in listOfOccurences:
   sum += occur
 emit (word, sum)
```

The map function splits the document into words and writes each word as a key and 1 as the value. MapReduce then collects all the pairs with the same key (word) and feeds them to the same reducer. Reducers sum all input values to compute the total count for the word. Both map and reduce are done in parallel over slices of the data, since MapReduce spans jobs for all nodes participating in the computations.

It is possible to code very different operations based on map and reduce, as shown in the SQL-like example given in [49]. It is also possible to define many iterations of map/reduce in the same application to implement more complex operations.

Scalable data processing and data management engines can be implemented on top of Hadoop, and Hadoop can be used for all sorts of computations and combined with all sorts of software to provide scalability in some stage of the computation. Hive, a data warehouse framework working on top of MapReduce and Hadoop, takes advantage of the flexibility of MapReduce to implement an SQL query processor. Hive allows users to specify SQL-like queries, transforms them into complex map/reduce execution plans and executes those against the datasets.

7.2. Scalable Data Processing on Hive

Hive is a data warehousing solution built on top of Hadoop and supporting queries written in an SQL-like language – HiveQL. The main objective of Hive is to apply relational database concepts and a subset of SQL to the context of Hadoop, simultaneously taking advantage of the scalability and flexibility of Hadoop.

One example scenario where Hive can be useful is to manage a data warehouse with thousands of tables, several hundred Terabytes and more than 100 users analysing and exploring data intensively for both reporting and ad-hoc analysis.

HiveQL is compiled into MapReduce jobs that are executed on Hadoop [72]. It is extensible, allowing users to add scripts customized for the MapReduce operations. HiveQL offers Data Definition Language (DDL) primitives for creating, dropping and modifying the structure of tables in a database. It also allows to load external data into tables. HiveQL Data Manipulation Language (DML) offers querying capabilities. Hive still has a set of limitations currently, in particular in what concerns update, delete and insert primitives, and dates and time are still treated as sequences.

Hive uses a MetaStore catalog to store metadata of a table. Its data model is similar to a database data model. Each Hive table corresponds to a folder in HDFS, the data of that table being serialized inside the folder. The infrastructure is extensible, users can customize serialization/ deserialization mechanisms. The system catalog stores the serialization format used for each table, which is used automatically during compilation and execution of queries. Tables can be partitioned, resulting in subdirectories whose name identifies the partitioning predicates.

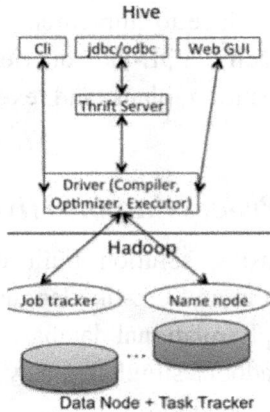

Figure 7.2 – Hive architecture

Figure 7.2 describes the architecture of Hive. It shows Hive and Hadoop. Hive offers as user interfaces both command line (Cli) and web interfaces, and also offers JDBC and ODBC interfaces for applications to use. The Thrift Server is a cross-language services framework, allowing servers developed in one language to be used by clients using other languages. The Driver manages compilation, optimization and execution of HiveQL statements. The compiler translates HiveQL into a job execution plan for MapReduce. Then the Driver submits individual jobs to MapReduce following the execution plan graph. Hive clients will launch MapReduce jobs on top of the HDFS, and Hive will interact directly with the HDFS to store data. Additionally, the Hive client accesses the Metastore server to manage the data schema.

7.3. Brief Results with Hive

We have run a set of queries from the Star-Schema Benchmark (SSB) [53] on two different systems. The first one was a low-end system with nodes made of low-end commodity PCs with an Intel Pentium 2.4 GHz microprocessor, 2GB of RAM and 100GB of disk space. The network bandwidth was only 100 Mbps. The second system was a high-end a multicore server with 40 GB of RAM, where each node was assigned two virtual processors, 8 GB of RAM and 125 GB of storage space. The following is an example of an SSB query that was run,

```
select sum(lo_revenue), d_year, p_brand
 from lineorder l join date d on l.lo_orderdate = d.d_datekey
join part p on l.lo_partkey = p.p_partkey
 join supplier s on l.lo_supkey = s.s_suppkey
 where p.p_category = 'MFGR#12' and s.s_region = 'AMERICA'
 group by d_year, p_brand
 order by d_year, p_brand;
```

We have installed a dataset of only 7.5GB in system A (it was not possible to run larger datasets in this setup) and compared Hive with a popular DBMS on those very low-end machines. On the high-end system we were able to run a 50 GB SSB dataset for the experiments. Figure 7.3 and Figure 7.4 show the speedup obtained in the low-end and the high-end systems respectively.

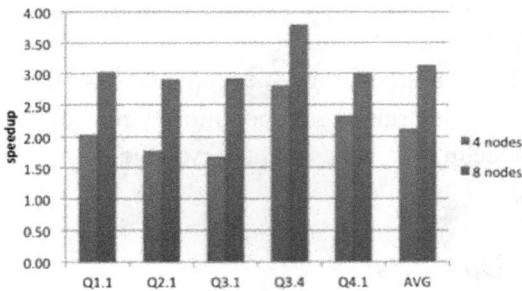

Figure 7.3 – Hive speedup on low-end nodes (7.5 GB)

The average speedup in the low-end system with 4 nodes was 2.2. This means that 4 nodes are added but the execution time is improved only by 2.1 times when compared with the one-node system. When 8 nodes are added, it is improved only 3.1 times. This also means that the improvement from adding more nodes decreased significantly as the number of nodes increased. This phenomenon is due to the increase in communication and housekeeping overhead that results from using more nodes, as well as the network bandwidth being only 100 Mbps.

The speedup for the high-end system is much better, about 3.3 in average with 4 nodes and 6.1 with 8 nodes. This is expected, since in this case the nodes are all installed in the same high-end server machine running virtual machines.

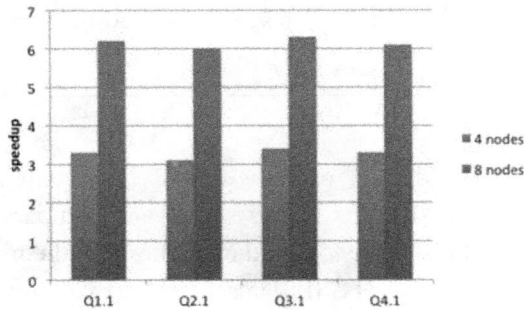

Figure 7.4 – Hive speedup on high-end nodes (50 GB)

These results show that, although it cannot achieve linear speedup, Hive was able to achieve a significant speedup when scaling on a high-end system. However, when running on commodity machines with a low-end network, the speedup is not satisfactory, due to the increased data exchange costs.

7.4. NoSQL Data Stores

When one first gets acquainted with the term "NoSQL", it is usual to ask what novelties does it bring, how it relates to DBMS, Hadoop and other data management and processing engines, and what it brings that is essentially different and relevant. We describe NoSQL systems conceptually in this section.

NoSQL data stores concentrate in storing and retrieving objects efficiently and in scaling. They do not attempt to offer the full power of SQL query language. Storage and retrieval of those objects is based on simple operations (get, put) indexed by a key field.

NoSQL systems offer efficient retrieval of multiple objects, frequently also adding the capability to apply filter conditions to retrieval (e.g.

retrieving only objects that obey some condition(s)). They are also designed to offer "full" horizontal scaling, usually also availability and fault tolerance, as objects are automatically routed to an appropriate server and replicated into multiple nodes for fault tolerance.

Figure 7.5 shows a typical "Distributed Hash Table" DHT-like organization for a NoSQL engine. The "PUT(key, value)" primitive stores a value indexed by key. The value can be anything. The "value GET(key)" returns the value associated with the key. Some other primitives also exist, including for instance range scans "scan(key1,key2)".

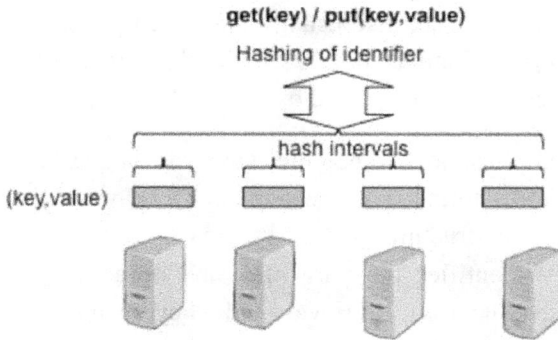

Figure 7.5 –Example Illustration of a NoSQL DHT Organization

NoSQL data stores have some other distinctive characteristics when compared to DBMSs. They offer data schema flexibility, meaning that the data does not have to conform to a specific schema. They also eliminate many overheads that are typical in DBMS, such as locking, logging, latching, or operating the data buffer. Additionally, they offer automatic scalability and guarantee access efficiency to individual objects, even in huge datasets (by scaling into multiple nodes and having efficient index over the key field to determine where to get the value from).

There are currently dozens of NoSQL engines, characterized as key-value stores, column-family stores and document stores. The Key-Value paradigm represents data as a set of tuples, each tuple having two parts: a

Key, which is used to partition the dataset and to locate tuples efficiently; and a Value, which is the information to be indexed by the value of the key.

Column-family stores organize data as column families, and column families can have any number of columns. Tuples can differ in terms of their attributes. This is the opposite of relational database engines, which are based on schemas where attributes of relations are defined in advance and every tuple has to agree to that design. Databases organized as column families are typically also key-value stores, since there is an indexing key field. The Value field is the set of column families. The column is a unit of storage of information identified by name and value. Column-family stores are also usually organized physically as columnar databases. In a columnar database the data is stored by columns (attributes) instead of being stored by rows.

As the name implies, document stores store the data as "documents", e.g. in JSON or XML formats. These documents may be grouped together and have a nested structure, just like typical JSON or XML documents. A unique key identifies the parts that are stored in the database for efficient retrieval later on. Retrieval by the key attribute is quite fast, but the documents can also be retrieved by any other attribute value. MongoDB is a well-known document store.

7.5. Exemplifying NoSQL with Cassandra

Cassandra is a fully distributed, no Single-Point-of-Failure NoSQL data store engine. Figure 7.6 shows a logical view of Cassandra's distributed storage mechanism. In the figure a client submits a put operation requesting the pair (k1, v1) to be stored. Node n5, which received the request, computes the hash of k1 and, depending on the hash ranges assigned to each node, directs the pair to be stored in one of the nodes and replicated into two other nodes for fault tolerance reasons. In this case, the pair is stored in nodes n2, n3 and n6.

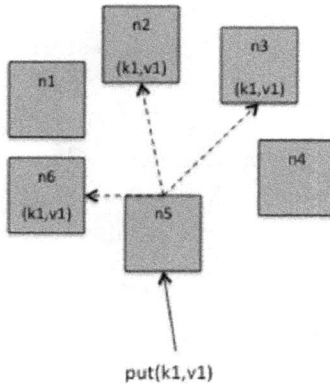

put(k1,v1)

Figure 7.6 – Cassandra Distributed Storage

Figure 7.7 shows an example of assignment of hash ranges to nodes. The assignment is done automatically, and re-adjusted also automatically when nodes enter or leave (readjustment requires data re-balancing, since key ranges are modified). Figure 7.8 shows two tuples indexed by the name attribute (Carlos and Miguel). The key attribute (name) is hashed (e.g. Carlos corresponds to md5 hash value 4f0745293) and the hashed value is compared with the hash-ranges in the table of Figure 7.7 to determine that 'Carlos' should be in node n1, and Miguel should be in node n6.

	hash start	hash end
n1	0x00000...	0x500000...
n2	0x50000...	0xa00000....
...	...	...
n6	0xe0000...	0xf0000...
...	...	...

Figure 7.7 –Hash Ranges

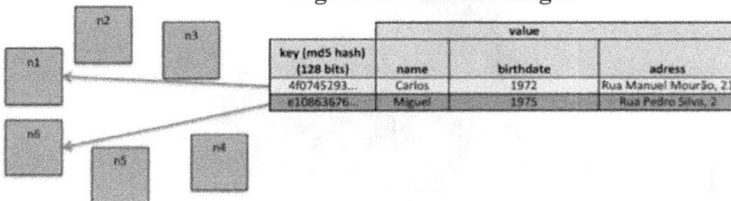

		value		
key (md5 hash) (128 bits)	name	birthdate	adress	
4f0745293...	Carlos	1972	Rua Manuel Mourão, 21	
e10863676...	Miguel	1975	Rua Pedro Silva, 2	

Figure 7.8 – Using Hash Ranges

7.6. Realtime Scalable Analytics

Figure 7.9 shows an infrastructure for scalable analytics that uses NoSQL and MapReduce. NoSQL data stores provide efficient and scalable storage and retrieval of tuples, even in huge datasets. It does not provide any complex computation capabilities. On the other hand, Hadoop and map-reduce provide complex computation capabilities with scalable processing, and allow tools and users to submit any computation to be automatically parallelized.

Realtime scalable analytics can be implemented using these two complementary solutions together. The NoSQL data store will store the data itself and benefit from scalability, fault tolerance and high retrieval and write efficiency. The Map-Reduce scalable platform will read and write from the NoSQL data store and will process the data efficiently, implementing analytics procedures. Several tools have been developed to automate many of the processing steps that may be needed, including for instance Hive (for SQL) and Mahout (for data mining).

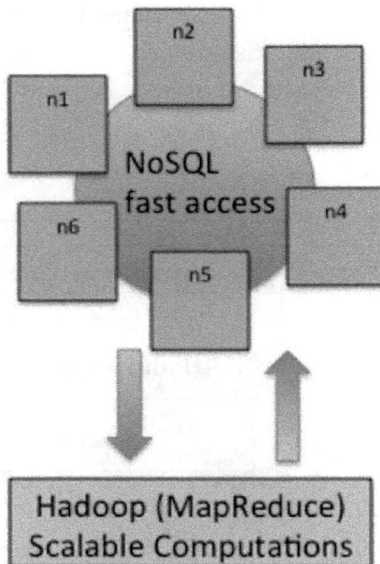

Figure 7.9 – Scalable Analytics using NoSQL

7.7. Conclusions

This chapter introduced modern scalability platforms and NoSQL engines. The conceptual architecture of those systems was presented, and we explained both how they work, how they can be used, and how they differ from traditional database management systems.

We described Hadoop, MapReduce and Hive. The combination of those technologies offers an approach to scale analytics processing to very large dataset sizes using any number of machines. The approach is easy to use and scalable, especially if ran in high-end servers.

We did not analyse how these technologies compare with top-performing parallel relational database management systems. This is done both qualitatively and quantitatively in [84, 88]. Parallel relational database engines are faster answering aggregation queries than Hive. This is because all details, from storage representation of the data to the algorithms that process complex operations, such as joins and aggregations, are fully optimized in a parallel relational database management system, while scalability frameworks such as Hadoop are designed for general-purpose scalable computations, on top of which the relational database processing mechanisms are added. Nonetheless, the Hive framework is easy to use, flexible, customizable and scales reasonably well. This has attracted the attention of big companies supplying data management engines, who increasingly add Hadoop and MapReduce products to their portfolio. It has also attracted the interest of integrator companies and their clients, who increasingly deploy those systems to have easily scalable and customizable solutions. In the future we expect to increasingly see integration of relational database technologies with MapReduce.

Pedro Furtado

Page intentionally left blank

Pedro Furtado

102

8. References

[1] Akal F., Böhm K., Schek H.-J.: "OLAP Query Evaluation in a Database Cluster: a Performance Study on Intra-Query Parallelism", East-European Conf. on Advances in Databases and Information Systems (ADBIS), Bratislava, Slovakia, 2002.

[2] Akinde, M. O., Bhlen, M. H., Johnson, T., Lakshmanan, L. V. S. and Srivastava, D. (2003) "Efficient OLAP query processing in distributed data warehouses", Information Systems 28, pp.111-135, Elsevier, 2003.

[3] Arumugam S., A. Dobra, C. M. Jermaine, N. Pansare, and L. Perez, "The DataPath system: a data-centric analytic processing engine for large data warehouses," Proceedings of the 2010 international conference on Management of data, pp. 519–530, 2010.

[4] Bellatreche L. and Boukhalfa K. "An Evolutionary Approach to Schema Partitioning Selection in a Data Warehouse", in International Conference on Data Warehousing and Knowledge Discovery, 2005.

[5] Bondi, André B. "Characteristics of scalability and their impact on performance". Proceedings of the second international workshop on Software and performance - WOSP '00. p. 195. ISBN 158113195X, (2000).

[6] Bruckner, R.M. List, B., Schiefer, J.: Striving towards near real-time data integration for data warehouses. In: Proceedings of DaWaK. (2002) 317-326.

[7] Chan C.-Y. and Ioannidis Y. E. (1998). Bitmap index design and evaluation. Proceedings of the International Conference on the Management of Data, pages 355-366, 1998.

[8] Chaudhuri, S. and Dayal, U. (1997). An overview of data warehousing and OLAP technology. SIGMOD Rec. 26, 1 (Mar. 1997), 65-74.

[9] Cooper B. F., Silberstein A., Tam E., Ramakrishnan R., Sears R. (2010). "Benchmarking cloud serving systems with YCSB". Proceedings of the 1st ACM Symposium on Cloud Computing, SoCC 2010, Indianapolis, Indiana, USA, June 10-11, 2010.

[10] Costa J., J. Cecílio, P. Martins, and P. Furtado, "ONE: a predictable and scalable DW model," in Proceedings of the 13th international conference on Data warehousing and knowledge discovery, Toulouse, France, 2011, pp. 1–13.

[11] Costa J., P. Martins, J. Cecílio, and P. Furtado, "A Predictable Storage Model for Scalable Parallel DW," in Fifteenth International Database Engineering and Applications Symposium (IDEAS 2011), Lisbon, Portugal, 2011.

[12] Costa J., Pedro Furtado: SPIN: Concurrent Workload Scaling over Data Warehouses. DaWaK 2013: 60-71: Data Warehousing and Knowledge Discovery - 15th International Conference, DaWaK 2013, Prague, Czech Republic, August 26-29, 2013. Proceedings. Springer 2013 Lecture Notes in Computer Science ISBN 978-3-642-40130-5.

[13] Costa, M. and Vieira, J. and Bernardino, J. and Furtado, P. and Madeira, H. , "A middle layer for distributed data warehouses using the DWS-AQA technique", VIII Jornadas de Ingeniería del Software y Bases de Datos, Alicante, Spain, November 2003.

[14] Costa. R., Furtado P. Data Warehouses in Grids with High QoS. In International Conference on Data Warehousing and Knowledge Discovery 2006: 207-217.

[15] DeWitt D., Gray J. (1992). "Parallel Database Systems: the Future of High Performance Database Processing". Communications of the ACM 35(6).

[16] Ferreira N., Furtado P, Real-Time Data Warehouse: A Solution and Evaluation, in International Journal on Business Intelligence and Data Mining, Elsevier, 2014.

[17] Ferreira N., Furtado P., "Near Real-Time with Traditional Data Warehouse Architectures: Factors and How-to", in 17th International Database Engineering and Applications Symposium, 2013.

[18] Furtado P. "Experimental Evidence on Partitioning in Parallel Data Warehouses". Proceedings of the ACM DOLAP 04 - Workshop of the International Conference on Information and Knowledge Management, Washington USA, Nov. 2004.

[19] Furtado P. "Workload-based Placement and Join Processing in Node-Partitioned Data Warehouses". Proceedings of the International Conference on Data Warehousing and Knowledge Discovery, 38-47, Zaragoza, Spain, September 2004.

[20] Furtado P., "Efficient and Robust Node-Partitioned Data Warehouses", in "Data Warehouses and OLAP: Concepts, Architectures and Solutions", ISBN 1-59904365-3 eds. R. Wrembel and C. Koncilia, Ideas Group, Inc, chapter IX, pp. 203-229.

[21] Furtado P., "A Survey of Parallel and Distributed Data Warehouses", International Journal of Data Warehousing and Mining, Volume 5, Number 2, 2009.

[22] Furtado P., Model and Procedure for Performance and Availability-wise Parallel Warehouses. In Distributed and Parallel Databases: Volume 25, Issue 1 (2009), Page 71, Spinger-Verlag. (B)

[23] Furtado P.: Replication in Node-Partitioned Data Warehouses. DDIDR2005 Workshop of VLDB 2005.

[24] Furtado, P. "Efficiently Processing Query-Intensive Databases over a Non-dedicated Local Network". Proceedings of the 19th International Parallel and Distributed Processing Symposium, Denver, Colorado, USA, May 2005.

[25] Ghazal, A., Rabl, T., Hu, M., Raab, F., Poess, M., Crolotte, A., Jacobsen, H.A.: BigBench: Towards an Industry Standard Benchmark for Big Data Analytics. In: SIGMOD. ACM Press, New York (2013).

[26] Giannikis G., G. Alonso, and D. Kossmann, "SharedDB: killing one thousand queries with one stone," Proc. VLDB Endow., vol. 5, no. 6, pp. 526–537, Feb. 2012.

[27] Han J., Y. Chen, G. Dong, J. Pei, B. W. Wah, J. Wang, and Y. D. Cai. Stream cube: An architecture for multi-dimensional analysis of

data streams. Distributed and Parallel Databases, 18(2):173–197, 2005.

[28] Hsiao H., DeWitt D. (1990). Chained Declustering: A New Availability Strategy for Multi-processor Database Machines. Intl. Conf. on Data Engineering, 1990.

[29] Hsiao H., DeWitt D. (1990b). Replicated Data Management in the Gamma Database Machine. Workshop on the Management of Replicated Data, 1990.

[30] Hsiao H., DeWitt D. J. (1991). A Performance Study of Three High Availability Data Replication Strategies. Procs of the Parallel and Distributed Systems, 1991.

[31] Hua, K. A. and Lee, C. (1990). "An Adaptive Data Placement Scheme for Parallel Database Computer Systems". Proceedings of the Sixteenth Very Large Data Bases Conference, 493-506, Brisbane, Queensland, Australia, August 1990.

[32] Hwang K., Hai Jin, Roy S. C. Ho: Orthogonal Striping and Mirroring in Distributed RAID for I/O-Centric Cluster Computing. IEEE Trans. Parallel Distrib. Syst. 13(1): 26-44 (2002).

[33] IBM DB2 Server www.ibm.com/db2.

[34] Iftikhar N. Integration, aggregation and exchange of farming device data: A high level perspective. In 2nd Conf. on the App. of Digital Information and Web Technologies, pages 14–19. IEEE, 2009.

[35] Iftikhar N., and T. B. Pedersen. An embedded database application for the aggregation of farming device data. In 16th European Conf. on Info. Sys. in Agriculture and Forestry, pages 51–59. Czech University of Life Sc., 2010.

[36] Iftikhar N., and T. B. Pedersen. Gradual data aggregation in multi-granular fact tables on resource-constrained systems. In 14th Int. Conf. on Knowledge-based Intelligent Information & Engineering Systems, pages 349–358. Springer, 2010.

[37] Iftikhar N., and T. B. Pedersen. Schema design alternatives for multi-granular data warehousing. In 21 Int. Conf. on Database and Expert Systems App., pages 111–125. Springer, 2010.

[38] Iftikhar N.,, Torben Bach Pedersen: A rule-based tool for gradual granular data aggregation. DOLAP 2011.

[39] Jain T., Rajasree S., Saluja S.: Refreshing Datawarehouse in Near Real-Time, International Journal of Computer Applications (0975 – 8887) Volume 46– No.18, May 2012.

[40] Kimbal, R., Caserta, J.: The data warehouse ETL toolkit: Practical techniques for extracting, cleaning, conforming, and delivering data. John Wiley & Sons (2004).

[41] Kimball, Ralph (1996). "The Data Warehouse Toolkit". Wiley. ISBN 0-471-15337-0.

[42] Kitsuregawa M., Tanaka H. and Motooka T. (1983). "Application of Hash to Database Machine and its Architecture". New Generation Computing, 63-74, 1(1).

[43] Lee E. K., Chandramohan A. Thekkath, Petal: Distributed Virtual Disks (1996). Proceedings of the Seventh International Conference on Architectural Support for Programming Languages and Operating Systems.

[44] Lerner A. and S. Lifschitz, "A Study of Workload Balancing Techniques on Parallel Join Algorithms," Proceedings of the International Conference on Parallel and Distributed Processing Techniques and Applications (PDPTA), pp:966-973, Las Vegas, EUA, July, 1998.

[45] Lerner A., "An Architecture for the Load-Balanced Parallel Join Operation in Shared-Nothing Environments," (in Portuguese), M.Sc. Dissertation, Computer Science Department, Pontificia Univ. Catolica do Rio de Janeiro, March, 1998.

[46] Lima, A. A. B., Mattoso, M., Valduriez, P.: OLAP Query Processing in a Database Cluster, Proc. 10th Euro-Par Conf., Pisa, Italy, 2004.

[47] Lima, A. A., Mattoso, M., Valduriez, P. Adaptive Virtual Partitioning for OLAP Query Processing in a Database Cluster", 19th Brasilian Simposium on Databases SBBD, 18-20 October 2004, Brasília, Brasil.

[48] Malewicz G., Austern M., Bik A., Dehnert J., Horn I., Leiser N., Czajkowski G., "Pregel: a system for large-scale graph processing", in Proceedings of the 2010 ACM SIGMOD International Conference on Management of data, Pages 135-146, ACM New York, NY, USA, 2010.

[49] MapReduce SQL-like example in Wikipedia, from http://en.wikipedia.org/wiki/MapReduce. [Accessed: 23-Aug-2014

[50] MapReduce word count example, from http://research.google.com/archive/mapreduce-osdi04-slides/index-auto-0004.html. [Accessed: 23-Aug-2014

[51] O'Neil P. and Graefe G. (1995). Multi-Table Joins Through Bitmapped Join Indices. SIGMOD Record, 24(3):8-11, 1995.

[52] Oracle, Best Practices for Real-time Data Warehousing, White Paper, 2012.

[53] Patrick O'Neil, Elizabeth (Betty) O'Neil, Xuedong Chen and Steve Revilak, The Star Schema Benchmark and Augmented Fact Table Indexing, Presentation at TPCTC (Transaction Processing Performance Council Technical Conference), Lyon, France, 2009.

[54] Patterson D.A., Gibson G. and Katz R. H. (1998). A case for redundant arrays of inexpensive disks (raid). Proceedings of the International Conference on Management of Data, 109-116, Chicago, USA, June 1998.

[55] Poess M., Nambiar R. O., Walrath D., (2007). "Why You Should Run TPC-DS: A Workload Analysis." VLDB '07, Proceedings of the 33rd international conference on Very Large Databases, pages 1138-1149, 2007.

[56] Ram, P., Do, L.: Extracting delta for incremental data Warehouse maintenance. In ICDE '00: Proceedings of the 16th International Conference on Data Engineering, page 220, Washington, DC, USA, 2000.

[57] Rao, J., Zhang c., Megiddo n., Lohman G. (2002). "Automating Physical Database Design in a Parallel Database". Proceedings of the ACM International Conference on Management of Data, 558-569, Madison, Wisconsin, USA, June 2002.

[58] Robinson I., Webber J., Eifrem E., "Graph Databases", June 2013, O'Reilly, ISBN 78-1-449-35626-2.

[59] Roddick. Schema vacuuming in temporal databases. IEEE Trans. on Knowledge and Data Engineering, 21(5):744–747, 2009.

[60] Rousopoulos R. (1998). Materialized Views and Data Warehouses. SIGMOD Record, 27(1):21-26, 1998.

[61] Shi, J., Bao, Y., Leng, F., and Yu, G.: "Study on log-based change data capture and handling mechanism in real-time data warehouse, " in CSSE '08: Proceedings of the 2008 International Conference on Computer Science and Software Engineering. Washington, DC, USA: IEEE Computer Society, 2008, pp. 478-481.

[62] Stöhr, Märtens T, Rahm H., Erhard (2002). "Dynamic Query Scheduling in Parallel Data Warehouses", Proceedings of Euro-Par 2002 Conference, Paderborn, August 2002.

[63] Stöhr, T, Märtens, H.; Rahm, E. Multi-Dimensional Database Allocation for Parallel Data Warehouses, Proc. 26th Intl. Conf. on Very Large Databases (VLDB), Cairo, Egypt, 2000.

[64] Stonebraker M., Gerhard A. Schloss: Distributed RAID - A New Multiple Copy Algorithm. International Conference on Data Engineering, 1990: 430-437.

[65] Tandem: NonStop SQL, A Distributed, High-Performance, High-Reliability Implementation of SQL. Workshop on High Performance Transactional Systems, CA USA, September 1987.

[66] Thomsen, C.S., Pedersen, T.B., Lehner, W.: RiTE: Providing on-demand data for right-time data warehousing. In: Proceedings of ICDE, Washington, DC, USA, IEEE Computer Society (2008) 456-465.

[67] Tilmann Rabl, Mohammad Sadoghi, Hans-Arno Jacobsen, Sergio G'omez-Villamor, Victor Muntes-Mulero, Serge Mankowskii. In PVLDB 5(12), 1724-1735, VLDB Endowment, 2012.

[68] TPC-H Benchmark, a Transactions Processing Council Benchmark, [Online]. http://www.tpc.org/tpc_h/, [Accessed: 7-Nov-2013].

[69] Unterbrunner P., G. Giannikis, G. Alonso, D. Fauser, and D. Kossmann, "Predictable performance for unpredictable workloads," Proc. VLDB Endow., vol. 2, pp. 706–717, Aug. 2009.

[70] Valduriez P. and Ozsu M. (1999). Principles of Parallel and Distributed Database Systems. Prentice-Hall, 3rd Ed., 1999.

[71] Vassiliadis, P., and Simitsis, A. 2008. Near Real Time ETL. In Springer journal Annals of Information Systems, Vol. 3, Special issue on New Trends in Data Warehousing and Data Analysis, ISBN 978-0-387-87430-2, Springer.

[72] Venner, J. "Pro Hadoop, Build scalable, distributed applications in the cloud", Apress, 2009, ISBN-13 (pbk): 978-1-4302-1942-2.

[73] Waas, F., Wrembel, R., Freudenreich, T., Thiele, M., Koncilia, C., Furtado, P.: On-Demand ELT Architecture for Right-Time BI: Extending the Vision. In: International Journal of Data Warehousing and Mining (IJDWM), volume 9 number 2 (2013).

[74] Yu, C. T. and Meng W. (1998). Principles of Database Query Processing for Advanced Applications. Morgan Kaufmann, 1998.

[75] Zhu, Y., An, L., Liu, S.: Data Updating and Query in Real-time Data Warehouse System, International Conference on Computer Science and Software Engineering, 2008.

[76] Zilio, D. C., Jhingran A, Padmanabhan S. (1994). "Partitioning Key Selection for a Shared-Nothing Parallel Database System". IBM Research Report RC 19820 (87739), 1994.

[77] Zuters, J.: Near Real-Time Data Warehousing with Multi-stage Trickle and Flip. In: Perspectives in Business Informatics Research, volume 90 of Lecture Notes in Business Information Processing, pages 73–82. Springer Berlin Heidelberg, 2011.

[78] Candea G., N. Polyzotis, and R. Vingralek, "A scalable, predictable join operator for highly concurrent data warehouses," Proc. VLDB Endow., vol. 2, pp. 277–288, Aug. 2009.

[79] Candea G., N. Polyzotis, and R. Vingralek, "Predictable performance and high query concurrency for data analytics," The VLDB Journal, vol. 20, no. 2, pp. 227–248, Apr. 2011.

[80] Costa, Pedro Furtado, "Data Warehouse Processing Scale-up for Massive Concurrent Queries with SPIN", in Transactions on Large Scale Data and Knowledge Centered Systems" (TLDKS), Springer, 2014.

[81] Harizopoulos S., V. Shkapenyuk, and A. Ailamaki, "QPipe: A Simultaneously Pipelined Relational Query Engine," Proceedings of the 2005 ACM SIGMOD international conference on Management of data, pp. 383–394, 2005.

[82] Iftikhar N., and T. B. Pedersen. Using a time granularity table for gradual granular data aggregation. In 14th East-European Conf. on Advances in Databases and Information Systems, pages 219–233. Springer, 2010.

[83] Norvag K.. Granularity reduction in temporal document databases. Information Systems, 31(2):134–147, 2006.

[84] Pavlo A., E. Paulson, A. Rasin, D. J. Abadi, D. J. DeWitt, S. Madden, and M. Stonebraker, "A comparison of approaches to large-scale data analysis," in SIGMOD '09: Proceedings of the 35th SIGMOD international conference on Management of data, New York, NY, USA, 2009, pp. 165-178.

[85] Pitarch Y., A. Laurent, M. Plantevit, and P. Poncelet. Multidimensional data stream summarization using extended tilted-timewindows. In Int. Conf. on Advanced Information Networking and Applications Workshops, pages 250–254. IEEE, 2009.

[86] Skyt, C. S. Jensen, and L. Mark. A foundation for vacuuming temporal databases. Data and Knowledge Engineering, 44(1):1–29, 2003.

[87] Skyt, C. S. Jensen, and T. B. Pedersen. Specification-based data reduction in dimensional data warehouses. Information Systems, 33(1):36–63, 2008.

[88] Stonebraker M., D. Abadi, D. J. DeWitt, S. Madden, E. Paulson, A. Pavlo, and A. Rasin, "MapReduce and Parallel DBMSs: Friends or Foes?," Communications of the ACM, vol. 53, iss. 1, pp. 64-71, 2010.

[89] Zhang, D. Gunopulos, V. J. Tsotras, and B. Seeger. Temporal and spatio-temporal aggregations over data streams using multiple time granularities. Information Systems, 28(1-2), 2003.

[90] Zukowski M., S. Héman, N. Nes, and P. Boncz, "Cooperative scans: dynamic bandwidth sharing in a DBMS," in Proceedings of the 33rd international conference on Very large data bases, Vienna, Austria, 2007, pp. 723–734.

[91] Williams M., Zhou S. (1998), "Data placement in parallel database systems". Parallel Database Techniques", IEEE Computer Society Press, California, USA, 203-219 1998.

[92] Epstein, Robert, Michael Stonebraker, & Eugene Wong, "Distributed Query Processing in a Relational Data Base System," Epstein, Robert, Michael Stonebraker, & Eugene Wong, 1978. In Proceedings of the 1978 ACM SIGMOD International Conference on Management of Data, 169–180. SIGMOD '78. New York, NY, USA: ACM.

[93] Graefe, Goetz, "Query Evaluation Techniques for Large Databases," Graefe, Goetz, 1993. ACM Comput. Surv. 25 (2) (June): 73–169.

[94] Shatdal, Ambuj, & Jeffrey F. Naughton, "Processing Aggregates in Parallel Database Systems", Shatdal, Ambuj, & Jeffrey F. Naughton, 1994. . Vol. Computer Sciences Technical Report #123. University of Wisconsin-Madison, Computer Sciences Department.

[95] Stöhr, Thomas, Holger Märtens, & Erhard Rahm, "Multi-Dimensional Database Allocation for Parallel Data Warehouses," Stöhr, Thomas, Holger Märtens, & Erhard Rahm, 2000. In Proceedings of the 26th International Conference on Very Large Data Bases, 273–284. VLDB '00. San Francisco, CA, USA: Morgan Kaufmann Publishers Inc.

[96] Bellatreche, L., K. Karlapalem, M. Mohania, & M. Schneider, "What Can Partitioning Do for Your Data Warehouses and Data Marts?," Bellatreche, L., K. Karlapalem, M. Mohania, & M. Schneider, 2000. In Database Engineering and Applications Symposium, 2000 International, 437–445.

[97] Yu, Clement T., Keh-Chang Guh, David Brill, & Arbee L. P. Chen, "Partition Strategy for Distributed Query Processing in Fast Local Networks," Yu, Clement T., Keh-Chang Guh, David Brill, & Arbee L. P. Chen, 1989. IEEE Trans. Softw. Eng. 15 (6) (June): 780–793.

[98] Liu, Chengwen, & C. Yu, "Validation and Performance Evaluation of the Partition and Replicate Algorithm," Liu, Chengwen, & C. Yu, 1992. In , Proceedings of the 12th International Conference on Distributed Computing Systems, 1992, 400–407.

[99] Mehta, Manish, & David J. DeWitt, "Data Placement in Shared-Nothing Parallel Database Systems," Mehta, Manish, & David J. DeWitt, 1997. The VLDB Journal 6 (1) (February): 53–72.

[100] Noaman, Amin Y., & Ken Barker, "A Horizontal Fragmentation Algorithm for the Fact Relation in a Distributed Data Warehouse," Noaman, Amin Y., & Ken Barker, 1999. In Proceedings of the Eighth International Conference on Information and Knowledge Management, 154–161. CIKM '99. New York, NY, USA: ACM.

[101] Ricardo Jorge Santos, Jorge Bernardino: Real-time data warehouse loading methodology. In International Database Engineering and Applications Symposium, IDEAS 2008: 49-58.

[102] Pavlo, Andrew, Erik Paulson, Alexander Rasin, Daniel J Abadi, David J DeWitt, Samuel Madden, & Michael Stonebraker, "A Comparison of Approaches to Large-Scale Data Analysis,", Proc. of the 35th SIGMOD International Conference on Management of Data. SIGMOD '09: 165–178.

[103] Furtado, Pedro. Efficient and Robust Node-Partitioned Data Warehouses. Pedro Furtado. Database Technologies: Concepts, Methodologies, Tools, and Applications, IGI Global, (2009).

[104] Jorge Bernardino, Henrique Madeira: Experimental Evaluation of a New Distributed Partitioning Technique for Data Warehouses. In International Database Engineering and Applications Symposium, IDEAS 2001: 312-321.

www.ingramcontent.com/pod-product-compliance
Lightning Source LLC
Chambersburg PA
CBHW061607220326
41598CB00024BC/3475

9 789892 050430